Editor
Dona Herweck Rice

Editorial Project Manager
Dona Herweck Rice

Editor-in-Chief
Sharon Coan, M.S. Ed.

Illustrator
Sue Fullam

Cover Artist
Barb Lorseyedi

Art Coordinator
Kevin Barnes

Imaging
Alfred Lau
Ralph Olmedo
Rosa C. See

Product Manager
Phil Garcia

Publisher
Rachelle Cracchiolo, M.S. Ed.

TIME FOR KIDS
Comprehension & Critical Thinking
LEVEL 3
Includes Document-Based Questions

Author

Jennifer Overend Prior, M. Ed.

Reading passages provided by *TIME For Kids* magazine.

Teacher Created Materials, Inc.
5301 Oceanus Drive
Huntington Beach, CA 92649
www.tcmpub.com
ISBN-0-7439-3373-7
©*2002 Teacher Created Materials, Inc.*
Made in U.S.A.
Reprinted, 2006

Teacher Created Materials
PUBLISHING

The classroom teacher may reproduce copies of materials in this book for classroom use only. The reproduction of any part for an entire school or school system is strictly prohibited. No part of this publication may be transmitted, stored, or recorded in any form without written permission from the publisher.

Table of Contents

Introduction

Comprehension is the primary goal of any reading task. Students who comprehend what they read have more opportunities in life as well as better test performance. Through the use of interesting grade-level nonfiction passages followed by exercises that require vital reading and thinking skills, *Comprehension and Critical Thinking* will help you to develop confident readers who can demonstrate their knowledge on standardized tests. In addition you will promote the comprehension necessary to form the basis for a lifetime of learning.

The articles in *Comprehension and Critical Thinking* present facts about the contemporary world as well as the past. A document-based question for each passage gives your students practice in the newest trend in standardized testing. The students respond to a critical-thinking question based on the information gleaned from a given document. This document is related to the passage it accompanies. Document-based questions show a student's ability to apply prior knowledge and his or her capacity to transfer knowledge to a new situation.

The activities are time-efficient, allowing students to practice these skills every week. To yield the best results, such practice must begin at the start of the school year.

Students will need to use test-taking skills and strategies throughout their lives. The exercises in *Comprehension and Critical Thinking* will guide your students to become better readers and test-takers. After practicing the exercises in this book, you will be pleased with your students' comprehension performance, not only on standardized tests, but with any expository text they encounter within the classroom and beyond its walls.

Readability

All of the passages have a 3.0-3.9 reading level based on the Flesch Kincaid Readability Formula. This formula determines the readability level by calculating the number of words, syllables, and sentences.

Preparing Students to Read Nonfiction Text

One of the best ways to prepare students to read expository text is to read a short selection aloud to them daily. Reading expository text aloud is critical to developing your students' ability to read it themselves. Since making predictions is another way to make students tap into their prior knowledge, read the beginning of a passage, then stop, and ask them to predict what might occur next. Do this at several points throughout your reading of the text. By doing this, over time you will find that your students' ability to make accurate predictions greatly increases.

Of course, talking about nonfiction concepts is also very important. Remember, however, that discussion can never replace reading aloud because people rarely speak using the vocabulary and complex sentence structures of written language.

Questions help students, especially struggling readers, to focus on what is important in a text. Also, remember the significance of wait time. Research has shown that the amount of time an educator waits for a student to answer after posing a question has a critical effect on learning. So, after you ask a student a question, silently count to five (or ten if you have a student who struggles to get his or her thoughts into words) before giving any additional prompts or redirecting the question to another student.

Introduction *(cont.)*

Bloom's Taxonomy

The questions that follow each passage in *Comprehension and Critical Thinking* assess all levels of learning by following Bloom's Taxonomy, a six-level classification system for comprehension questions devised by Benjamin Bloom in 1956. The questions that follow each passage are always presented in order, progressing from knowledge to evaluation.

The skills listed for each level are essential to keep in mind when teaching comprehension to ensure that your students reach the higher levels of thinking. Use this classification to form your own questions whenever your students listen to or read material.

Level 1: Knowledge—Students recall information or find requested information in an article. They show memory of dates, events, places, people, and main ideas.

Level 2: Comprehension—Students understand information. This means that they can find information that is stated in a different way than the question. It also means students can rephrase or restate information in their own words.

Level 3: Application—Students apply their knowledge to a specific situation. They may be asked to do something new with the knowledge.

Level 4: Analysis—Students break things into their component parts and examine those parts. They notice patterns in information.

Level 5: Synthesis—Students do something new with the information. They pull knowledge together to create new ideas. They generalize, predict, plan, and draw conclusions.

Level 6: Evaluation—Students make judgments and assess value. They form an opinion and defend it. They can also understand another person's viewpoint.

Practice Suggestions

Do the first few passages and related questions with the whole class. Demonstrate your own metacognitive processes by thinking aloud about how to figure out an answer. This means that you essentially tell your students your thoughts as they come to you. For example, suppose the question is the following: "What would have happened to the baby dinosaurs if mud had not preserved them?" Tell the students all your thoughts as they occur to you, for example: "What happens to most animals' bodies when they die? Not every animal's body becomes a fossil. The mud is what preserved the dinosaurs' bodies. So, if the mud hadn't covered them, the bodies would probably have deteriorated or rotted away."

Introduction *(cont.)*

Short-answer Questions

Many of the questions require short answers. The students are asked to use information from the article to summarize, draw conclusions, identify hidden meanings, etc. The student should support his or her ideas and opinions when necessary.

Document-based Questions

It is especially important to guide your students in how to understand, interpret, and respond to the document-based questions. For these questions, in order to formulate a response the students will have to rely on their prior knowledge and common sense in addition to the information provided in the document. Again, the best way to teach this is to demonstrate through thinking aloud how to figure out an answer. Since these questions are usually interpretive, you can allow for some variation in student responses.

The more your students practice, the more competent and confident they will become. Plan to have the class do every exercise in *Comprehension and Critical Thinking*. If you have some students who cannot read the articles independently, allow them to read with a partner, then work through the comprehension questions alone. Eventually all students must practice reading and answering the questions independently. Move to this stage as soon as possible. For the most effective practice sessions, follow these steps:

1. Have the students read the text silently and answer the questions.

2. Have the students exchange papers to correct each other's multiple choice section.

3. Collect all the papers to score the short-answer question and the document-based question portion.

4. Return the papers to their owners and discuss how the students determined their answers.

5. Refer to the exact wording in the passage.

6. Point out how students had to use their background knowledge to answer certain questions.

7. Discuss how a child should explain his or her stance in each short-answer question.

8. Discuss the document-based question thoroughly.

Scoring the Practice Passages

With the students, use the "number correct" approach to scoring the practice passages, especially since this coincides with the student achievement graph on page 109. However, for your own records and to share with the parents, you may want to keep track of numeric scores for each student. If you choose to do this, do not write the numeric score on the paper.

Introduction *(cont.)*

Standardized Test Success

One of the key objectives of *Comprehension and Critical Thinking* is to prepare your students to get the best possible scores on the reading portion of standardized tests. A student's ability to do well on traditional standardized tests in comprehension requires these factors:

- a large vocabulary
- test-taking skills
- the ability to cope with stress effectively

Test-taking Skills

Every student in your class needs instruction in test-taking skills. Even fluent readers and logical thinkers will perform better on standardized tests if you provide instruction in the following areas.

Understanding the question: Teach students to break down the question to figure out what is really being asked of them. This book will prepare them for the kinds of questions they will encounter on standardized tests.

Concentrating just on what the text says: Show students how to restrict their response to just what is asked. When you go over the practice passages, ask your students to show where they found the correct response in the text.

Ruling out distracters in multiple-choice answers: Teach students to look for the key words in a question and look for those specific words to find the information in the text. They also need to know that they may have to look for synonyms for the key words.

Maintaining concentration: Use classroom time to practice this in advance. Reward students for maintaining concentration. Explain to them the purpose of this practice and the reason why concentration is so essential.

Practice environmental conditions throughout the year in order to acclimate your students to the testing environment. For example, if your students' desks are usually together, have students move them apart whenever you practice so it won't feel strange on the test day.

Some other ideas for "setting the stage" whenever you practice include the following:

- Put a "Testing—Do Not Disturb" sign on the door.
- Require no talking, active listening, and following directions during practice sessions.
- Provide a small strip of construction paper for each student to use as a marker.
- Give each student two sharpened pencils and have a back-up supply handy. Tell the students to raise a broken pencil, and you will immediately provide them with a new one.

Introduction *(cont.)*

Coping with Stress

Teach students to recognize their apprehension and other stressful feelings associated with testing. Give students some suggestions for handling stress, such as taking a deep breath and stretching.

At the beginning of the school year start talking about good habits like getting enough rest, having a good breakfast, and daily exercise. Enlist parental support by sending home a letter encouraging parents to start these good habits right away.

Remember to let students stretch and move around between tests. Provide a physical release by running in place or playing "Simon Says" as a stress-buster during practice sessions throughout the year as well as on the test day.

Build confidence throughout the school year by using the practice passages in this book. Do not include the passage scores in the students' class grades. Instead, encourage your students by having them complete the achievement line graph on page 109, showing how many questions they answered correctly for each practice passage. Seeing their scores improve or stay consistently high over time will provide encouragement and motivation.

On the test day, promote a relaxed, positive outlook. Tell your students to visualize doing really well. Remind them that since they have practiced so much, they are thoroughly prepared.

Teaching Nonfiction Comprehension Skills

Nonfiction comprehension encompasses many skills that develop with a lot of practice. The following information offers you a brief overview of how to teach the crucial skills of recognizing text structure, visualizing, summarizing, and learning new vocabulary. This information is designed for your use with other classroom materials, not the practice passages in *Comprehension and Critical Thinking*.

You will find many of these skills in scope-and-sequence charts and standards for reading comprehension:

- recognizes stated main idea
- identifies details
- determines sequence
- recalls details
- labels parts
- summarizes
- identifies time sequence
- describes character
- retells information in own words

- classifies, sorts into categories
- compares and contrasts
- makes generalizations
- draws conclusions
- recognizes text organization
- predicts outcome and consequences
- experiences an emotional reaction to a text
- recognizes facts
- applies information to a new situation

Introduction *(cont.)*

Typical Comprehension Questions

Teaching the typical kinds of standardized test questions gives students an anticipation framework and helps them learn how to comprehend what they read. It also boosts their test scores. The questions generally found on standardized reading comprehension tests are as follows:

Facts—questions based on exactly what the text states: who, what, when, where, why, and how many

Sequence—questions based on order: what happened first, last, and in between

Conditions—questions asking students to compare, contrast, and find the similarities and differences

Summarizing—questions that require students to restate, paraphrase, choose main ideas, conclude, and select a title

Vocabulary—questions based on word meaning, synonyms and antonyms, proper nouns, words in context, technical words, geographical words, and unusual adjectives

Outcomes—questions that ask readers to draw upon their own experiences or prior knowledge, which means that students must understand cause and effect, consequences, and implications

Opinion—questions that ask the author's intent and require the use of inferencing skills

Document-based—questions that require students to analyze information from a source document to draw a conclusion or form an opinion

Introduction (cont.)

Teaching Text Structure

Students lacking in knowledge of text structure are at a distinct disadvantage; yet this skill is sometimes overlooked in instruction. When referring to a piece to locate information to answer a question, understanding structure allows students to locate quickly the right area in which to look. Students also need to understand text structure in order to make predictions and improve overall comprehension.

Some children have been so immersed in print that they have a natural understanding of structure. For instance, they realize that the first sentence of a paragraph often contains the main idea, followed by details about that idea. But many students need direct instruction in text structure. The first step in this process is making certain that students know the way that authors typically present ideas in writing. This knowledge is a major asset for students.

Transitional paragraphs join together two paragraphs to make the writing flow. Most transitional paragraphs do not have a main idea. In all other paragraph types, there is a main idea, even if it is not stated. In the following examples the main idea is italicized. In order of frequency, the four types of expository paragraph structures are as follows:

1. **The main idea is often the first sentence of a paragraph. The rest of the paragraph provides the supporting details.**

   Clara Barton, known as America's first nurse, was a brave and devoted humanitarian. While caring for others, she was shot at, got frostbitten fingers, and burned her hands. She had severe laryngitis twice and almost lost her eyesight. Yet she continued to care for the sick and injured until she died at the age of 91.

2. **The main idea may fall in the center of the paragraph, surrounded on both sides by details.**

   The coral have created a reef where more than 200 kinds of birds and about 1,500 types of fish live. *In fact, Australia's Great Barrier Reef provides a home for many interesting animals.* These include sea turtles, giant clams, crabs, and crown-of-thorns starfish.

3. **The main idea comes at the end of the paragraph as a summary of the details that came before.**

   Each year Antarctica spends six months in darkness, from mid-March to mid-September. The continent is covered year-round by ice, which causes sunlight to reflect off its surface. It never really warms up. In fact, the coldest temperature ever recorded was in Antarctica. *Antarctica has one of the harshest environments in the world.*

Introduction *(cont.)*

4. **The main idea is not stated in the paragraph and must be inferred from the details given. This paragraph structure is the most challenging for primary students.**

The biggest sea horse ever found was over a foot long. Large sea horses live along the coasts of New Zealand, Australia, and California. Smaller sea horses live off the coast of Florida, in the Caribbean Sea, and in the Gulf of Mexico. The smallest adult sea horse ever found was only one half-inch long!

In this example, the implied main idea is that sea horses' sizes vary based on where they live.

Some other activities that will help your students understand text structure include the following:

Color code: While reading text, have your students use different colored pencils or highlighters to color code important elements such as the main idea (red), supporting details (yellow), causes (green) and effects (purple), facts (blue) and opinions (orange). When they have finished, ask them to describe the paragraph's structure in their own words.

Search the text: Teach students to identify the key words in a question and look specifically for those words in the passage. Then, when you discuss a comprehension question with the students, ask them, "Which words will you look for in the text to find the answer? If you can't find the words, can you find synonyms? Where will you look for the words?"

Signal words: There are specific words used in text that indicate, or signal, that the text has a cause and effect, sequence, or comparison structure. Teaching your students these words will greatly improve their ability to detect text structure and increase their comprehension.

These Signal Words	Indicate
since, because, caused by, as a result, before and after, so, this led to, if/then, reasons, brought about, so that, when/then, that's why	cause and effect The answer to "Why did it happen?" is a cause. The answer to "What happened?" is an effect.
first, second, third, next, then, after, before, last, later, since then, now, while, meanwhile, at the same time, finally, when, at last, in the end, since that time, following, on (date), at (time)	sequence
but, even if, even though, although, however, instead, not only, unless, yet, on the other hand, either/or, as well as, "–er" and "–st" words (such as better, best, shorter, tallest, bigger, smallest, most, worst)	

Introduction (cont.)

Teaching Visualization Skills

Visualization—seeing the words of a text as mental images in the mind—is a significant factor setting apart proficient readers from low-achieving ones. Studies have shown that the ability to generate vivid images while reading strongly correlates with a person's comprehension of text. However, research has also revealed that *20 percent of all children do not visualize or experience sensory images when reading.* These children are automatically handicapped in their ability to comprehend text, and they are usually the students who avoid and dislike reading because they never connect to text in a personal, meaningful way.

Active visualization can completely engross a reader in text. You have experienced this when you just could not put a book down, and you stayed up all night just to finish it. Skillful readers automatically weave their own memories into text as they read to make personalized, lifelike images. In fact, every person develops a unique interpretation of any text. This personalized reading experience explains why most people prefer a book to its movie.

Visualization is not static; unlike photographs, these are "movies in the mind." Mental images must constantly be modified to incorporate new information as it is disclosed by the text. Therefore, your students must learn how to revise their images if they encounter information that requires them to do so.

Sensory imaging—employing any of the other senses besides sight—is closely related to visual imaging. It too has been shown to be crucial to the construction of meaning during reading. This is because the more senses that are employed in a task, the more neural pathways are built, resulting in more avenues to access information. You have experienced sensory imaging when you could almost smell the smoke of the forest fire, taste the sizzling bacon, or laughed along with a character as you read. Sensory imaging connects the reader personally and intimately to the text and breathes life into words.

Since visualization is a challenging skill for one out of every five students to develop, begin with simple *fictional* passages to scaffold their attempts and promote success. After your students have experienced success with visualization and sensory imaging in literature, they are ready to employ these techniques in nonfiction text.

Visualization has a special significance in nonfiction text. The technical presentation of ideas in nonfiction text coupled with new terms and concepts often overwhelm and discourage students. Using visualization can help them to move beyond these barriers. As an added benefit, people who create mental images display better long-term retention of factual material.

Clearly there are important reasons to teach visualization and sensory imaging skills to your students. But perhaps the most compelling reason is this: Visualizing demands active involvement, turning passive students into *active* constructors of meaning.

Introduction (cont.)

Doing Think-Alouds

It is essential for you to introduce visualization by doing think-alouds to describe your own visualization of text. To do this, read aloud the first one or two lines of a passage and describe what images come to your mind. Be sure to include *details that were not stated in the text,* such as the house has two stories and green shutters. Then read the next two lines and explain how you add to or otherwise modify your image based on the new information provided by the text.

When you are doing a think-aloud for your class, be sure to do the following:

- Explain how your images help you to better understand the passage.
- Describe details, being sure to include some from your own schema.
- Mention the use of your senses—the more the better.
- Describe your revision of the images as you read further and encounter new information.

Teaching Summarizing and Paraphrasing

Summarizing informational text is a crucial skill for students to master. It is also one of the most challenging. Summarizing means pulling out only the essential elements of a passage—just the main idea and supporting details. Research has shown that having students put information into their own words causes it to be processed more thoroughly. Thus, paraphrasing increases both understanding and long-term retention of material. Information can be summarized through such diverse activities as speaking, writing, drawing, or creating a project.

The basic steps of summarizing are as follows:

- Look for the paragraph's main idea sentence; if there is none, create one.
- Find the supporting details, being certain to group all related terms or ideas.
- Record information that is repeated or restated only once.
- Put the summary together into an organized format.

Scaffolding is of critical importance. Your students will need a lot of modeling, guided practice, and small-group or partner practice before attempting to summarize independently. All strategies should be done as a whole group and then with a partner several times before letting the students do it on their own. Encourage the greatest transfer of knowledge by modeling each strategy's use in multiple content areas.

Teaching Vocabulary

In the early years, students may start seeing words in print that they may have never met before in either print or oral language. As a result, these students need direct instruction in vocabulary to make real progress toward becoming readers who can independently access expository text. Teaching the vocabulary that occurs in a text significantly improves comprehension. Since students encounter vocabulary terms in science, social studies, math, and language arts, strategies for decoding and understanding new words must be taught throughout the day.

Introduction (cont.)

Students' vocabularies develop following this progression: listening, speaking, reading, and writing. This means that a child understands a word when it is spoken to him long before he uses it in his own speaking. The child will also understand the word when he reads it before he will attempt to use it in his own writing. Each time a child comes across the same word, his or her understanding of that word deepens. Research has shown that vocabulary instruction has the most positive effect on reading comprehension when students encounter the words multiple times. That is why the best vocabulary instruction requires students to use new words in writing and speaking as well as in reading.

Teaching vocabulary can be both effective and fun, especially if you engage the students' multiple modalities (listening, speaking, reading, and writing). In addition, instruction that uses all four modalities is most apt to reach every learner.

The more experience a child has with language, the stronger his or her vocabulary base. Therefore, the majority of vocabulary activities should be done as whole-group or small-group instruction. In this way children with a limited vocabulary can learn from their peers' knowledge base and will find vocabulary activities less frustrating. Remember, too, that a picture is worth a thousand words. Whenever possible provide a picture of a new vocabulary word.

Selecting Vocabulary Words to Study

Many teachers feel overwhelmed when teaching vocabulary because they realize that it is impossible to thoroughly cover all students' unknown words. Do not attempt to study every unknown word. Instead, choose the words from each selection wisely. Following these guidelines will result in an educationally sound vocabulary list:

- First choose words that are critical to the article's meaning.

- Then choose conceptually difficult words.

- Finally choose words with the greatest utility value—those that you anticipate the children will see more often (*e.g.*, choose *anxious* rather than *appalled*).

These suggestions are given for teaching nonfiction material in general. *Do not select and preteach vocabulary from these practice passages.* You want to simulate real test conditions in which the children would have no prior knowledge of any of the material in any of the passages.

Elements of Effective Vocabulary Instruction

Vocabulary instruction is only effective if children permanently add the concepts to their knowledge base. Research has shown that the most effective vocabulary program includes contextual, structural, and classification strategies. You can do this by making certain that your vocabulary instruction includes the following elements:

- using context clues

- knowing the meaning of affixes (prefixes, suffixes) and roots

- introducing new words as synonyms and antonyms of known words

Introduction *(cont.)*

Using Context Clues

Learning vocabulary in context is important for two reasons. First, it makes children become active in determining word meanings, and second, it transfers into their lives by offering them a way to figure out unknown words in their independent reading. If you teach your students how to use context clues, you may eventually be able to omit preteaching any vocabulary that is defined in context (so long as the text is written at your students' independent level). There are five basic kinds of context clues.

1. **Definition:** The easiest case is when the definition is given elsewhere in the sentence or paragraph.

    example: The ragged, *tattered* dress hung from her shoulders.

2. **Synonym:** Another simple case is when a synonym or synonymous phrase is immediately used.

    example: Although she was fat, her *obesity* never bothered her until she went to middle school.

3. **Contrast:** The meaning may be implied through contrast to a known word or concept. Be alert to these words that signal contrast: although, but, however, even though.

    example: Although Adesha had always been *prompt*, today he was 20 minutes late.

4. **Summary:** Another form is summary, which sums up a list of attributes.

    example: Tundra, desert, grassland, and rain forest are four of the Earth's *biomes*.

5. **Mood:** Sometimes the meaning can be grasped from the mood of the larger context in which it appears. The most difficult situation is when the meaning must be inferred with few other clues.

    example: Her *shrill* voice was actually making my ears hurt.

Your general approach to building vocabulary should include the following:

Brainstorming: Students brainstorm a list of words associated with a familiar word, sharing everyone's knowledge and discussing unfamiliar words thoroughly.

Semantic mapping: Students sort the brainstormed words into categories, often creating a visual organization tool—such as a graphic organizer or word web—to depict the relationships.

Feature analysis: You provide key features and a list of terms in a chart, such as a semantic matrix or Venn diagram. Have students identify the similarities and differences between the items.

Synonyms and antonyms: Introducing both synonyms and antonyms for the terms you study provides a structure for meaning and substantially increases your students' vocabulary rapidly.

Analogies: Analogies are similar to synonyms but require higher-level thinking. The goal is to help students identify the relationship between words. Analogies appear on standardized tests in the upper elementary grades.

    example: Bark is to tree as skin is to <u>human</u>.

Introduction *(cont.)*

Word affixes: Studying common prefixes and suffixes will help students deduce new words, especially in context. Teach students to ask, "Does this look like any other word I know? Can I find any word parts I know? Can I figure out the meaning based on its context?"

Important Affixes for Primary Grades

Prefix	Meaning	Example	Suffix	Meaning	Example
un	not	unusual	**-s or -es**	more than one	cars; tomatoes
re	again	redo	**-ed**	did an action	moved
in, im	not	impassable	**-ing**	doing an action	buying
dis	opposite	disassemble	**-ly**	like, very	usually
non	not	nonathletic	**-er**	a person who	farmer
over	too much	overcook	**-ful**	full of	respectful
mis	bad	misrepresent	**-or**	a person who	creator
pre	before	prearrange	**-less**	without	harmless
de	opposite	decompose	**-er**	more	calmer
under	less	underachieve	**-est**	most	happiest

Dino Eggs by the Dozen

It was more than 70 million years ago. A group of female dinosaurs roamed along a riverbank in South America. They were going to lay their eggs there. There were thousands of eggs! One by one, the baby dinosaurs started to hatch.

Then a giant flood washed over the land. They were lost forever.

Well, not quite forever. In November 1998, a group of scientists uncovered something. They found the eggs and babies.

Scientists were in a field. It was covered with rocks the size of grapefruits. They took a closer look. The "rocks" were really dinosaur eggs. "There were thousands of eggs all over the place," says Luis Chiappe, a team leader.

The eggs belonged to small dinosaurs. They had long necks and ate plants. They are called titanosaurs.

Of course, all of these dinosaurs were not really small. An adult titanosaur was more than 50 feet long. Babies were about 15 inches long. That's "the size of a small poodle," says Chiappe.

The flood buried the eggs in mud. The mud helped preserve the babies still inside the eggshells. One egg held 32 teeth. Each tooth is small enough to fit inside this capital "O." Others held patches of scaly skin.

Chiappe and his team returned to the area. They hoped to answer more questions. They wanted to know whether the mama dinosaurs made careful nests or laid their eggs just anywhere. With so many eggs yet to be studied, those answers may be just waiting to hatch.

Dino Eggs by the Dozen *(cont.)*

Directions: Answer these questions. You may look at the story.

1. On what continent were the dinosaurs roaming the riverbank?

2. Why were the baby dinosaurs "lost forever"?

3. Why weren't the eggs and babies really lost forever?

4. Why do you think the scientists want to learn more about these dinosaurs?

5. How was this discovery helpful to scientists?

6. What would have happened to the babies if mud had not preserved them?

7. How were the eggs similar to grapefruits?

8. If the floods had not come, what would have happened to these dinosaurs?

9. Explain the importance of this discovery to scientists.

Dino Eggs by the Dozen *(cont.)*

Directions: Look at the picture. Answer the questions.

titanosaur

1. Look at the head and body pictures of the titanosaur. How do you think scientists were able to tell that it was a plant eater?

2. An adult titanosaur was probably about 50 feet long. Why do you think scientists say this is a small dinosaur?

Directions: Read the story.

Racing a Tornado!

The Saturday Maria and I had picked for our 50-mile bike ride seemed perfect. We set out at 7 a.m. in beautiful spring weather. The air smelled fresh and clean. The sun shone brightly and birds sang in the trees along the roadside. Wildflowers looked like flames of color waving in the fields. At 10:30 when we stopped for a break, we both felt terrific. As we rested, though, a brisk wind sprang up. That was when our perfect day began to change.

By noon, we knew a serious thunderstorm was blowing our way. A towering bank of dark clouds had rolled up out of the southwest. A stinging wind burned our faces. Stopping under a big oak tree, we frowned at each other with worry. There was no way to stay out of the storm. We would have to wait it out, but where?

Then things went from bad to worse. The temperature dropped suddenly. I looked up and saw that the sky now had a dark-greenish cast. Trees and crops were bent over by the wind and no animals were in sight.

Then a blue car pulled alongside our bikes. The driver ordered, "Get in!" She looked frightened and we must have, too. We did as she said just as the hail started. Chunks of ice the size of golf balls pounded the windshield and dented the hood. Our tree would never have protected us, I thought, and silently thanked our rescuer.

She sped northward with a determined look on her face. Could she outrun this storm? Maria and I looked backward at the black sky. That's when we saw it. Maria screamed. I yelled, "Tornado!" The funnel didn't look real, yet I knew it had to be. It was so close that I could see tree limbs, doors, and all sorts of other stuff that this monster had swallowed and was spinning around.

My heart had moved up to my throat and was beating so hard I thought it would leap from my body. I had never been so terrified. We would never outrun the tornado! It seemed to be moving closer. The driver turned to us and said calmly, "We'll get through this. There's an overpass ahead. We'll pull in there for protection." She explained that we must lie flat in the lowest protected area.

Once we parked, we leapt from the car and lay pressed up against the concrete wall of the overpass. Not a minute too soon. Before I could count to twenty, a roaring surrounded us. It sounded like a freight train passing overhead. Then, suddenly, it was over. We had made it by the skin of our teeth.

Some trees were uprooted. Tree branches and flowers were scattered all over. Yet everything was calm and quiet.

We got to a phone and called home. Our parents had been worried sick. But soon we were all laughing with relief. We were shaken but excited. What a story I would have to tell at school!

Racing a Tornado! *(cont.)*

Directions: Answer these questions. You may look at the story.

1. What terrible thing did the kids encounter?

2. Why was there no way for them to stay out of the storm?

3. What were the signs that a storm was coming?

4. How did the kids know that the driver was frightened?

5. Compare the differences between a thunderstorm and a tornado.

6. What do you think would have happened if the kids had not met the driver?

7. What do you think happened to the area where the tornado hit?

8. Summarize the article using only three sentences.

 ©Teacher Created Materials, Inc.

Racing a Tornado! *(cont.)*

Directions: Tornadoes happen in many places in the United States. Tornado Alley, the circled area, is the place where they occur most often. Look at the map and then answer the questions.

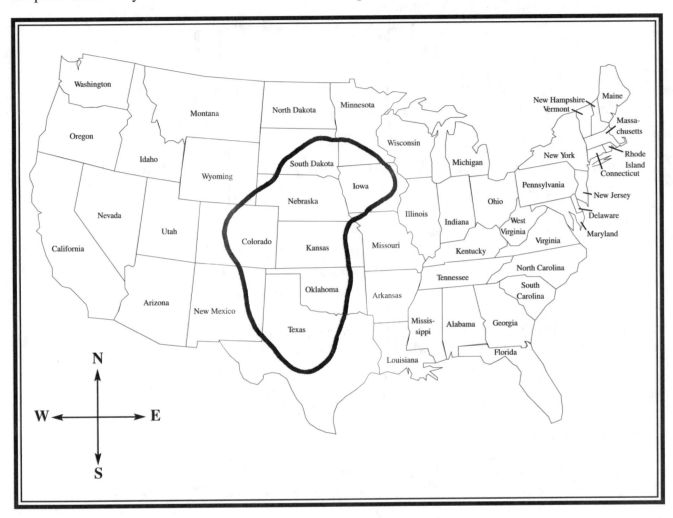

1. How does this map help you to better understand the article?

2. If you live in Colorado, how likely are you to experience a tornado?

3. Do you think that tornadoes begin over the ocean? Why or why not?

4. Why do you think this area is called an alley?

Directions: Read the story.

A Spooky Friend

The sun sets below the horizon. The wind blows leaves around your feet. Suddenly a vampire bat swoops down to suck your blood!

OK, catch your breath. Scary stories about bats have been around for a long time. In real life, bats hardly ever hurt people. These furry, flying mammals are really very helpful.

Bats eat bugs. Bugs hurt farmers' crops. Bats feast on insect pests and help farmers. There are 20 million Mexican free-tailed bats near San Antonio, Texas. They eat up 250 tons of insects every night! Bats also snack on flies and mosquitoes that can get in your food.

Bats help the desert, too. They carry pollen from cactus to cactus and spread the seeds around. Birds and other desert animals depend on cactus plants for food.

Actually bats should be afraid of people. Today many kinds of bats are endangered.

Some people fear bats. They burn them out of caves or bury them inside mines. Thomas Kunz is a biologist. He says, "They think every bat is a vampire bat, and they kill all they can find."

A Spooky Friend (cont.)

Directions: Answer these questions. You may look at the story.

1. What do bats eat?

2. How many tons of insects can bats eat in a night?

3. How do bats help farmers?

4. Describe several helpful things that bats do.

5. If the bats in Texas eat 250 tons of insects a night, how many would they eat in three nights?

6. Why shouldn't you be afraid of bats?

7. If all bats disappeared, how would that hurt the environment?

8. How would you convince someone that bats are helpful and not harmful?

A Spooky Friend *(cont.)*

Directions: Look at the diagram. Answer the questions.

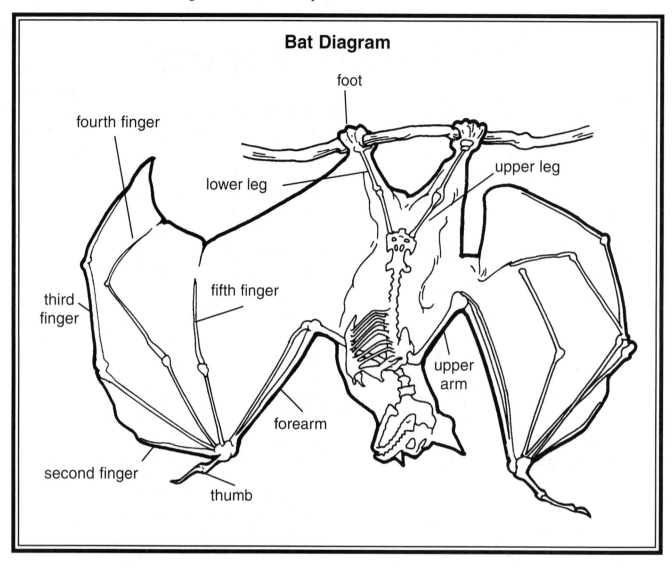

Bat Diagram

foot

fourth finger

upper leg

lower leg

fifth finger

third finger

upper arm

forearm

second finger

thumb

1. How does this diagram help you to better understand the bat?

2. What are three things you can learn from this diagram that are not mentioned in the article?

3. How could this diagram be used to teach a person about bats?

4. After looking at this diagram, what are three questions that you have about bats?

Directions: Read the story.

No Helmet? Pay Up!

"Stop, kid! Get off that bike!" Bike riders in Florida must now wear helmets. They might even have to pay $17 for breaking the law!

Many states have passed helmet laws. In Florida the law applies to all kids under 16. Some helmet laws give kids a break. Kids who can prove that they have bought helmets don't have to pay their tickets.

Why are some states getting so tough about helmets? Think of the last time you fell off your bike. Did you bruise your knee? Did you scrape your elbow? Did you hit your head? Thousands of kids tumble off bicycles every year, and many suffer serious injuries. A head injury can be much worse. A very bad head injury can kill you. But helmets help. Bike helmets lower the risk of head injury by 85%.

Simon Crider, 11, knows how important a helmet can be. In 1995, he was riding his bike. He hit a rock and flew over his handlebars. His head hit the pavement, and his helmet cracked. Luckily, only his helmet got damaged.

Still a lot of kids are not crazy about wearing helmets. A bicycle-safety leader in Florida says, "A big part of it is the 'dork' factor. Some kids just don't think helmets are cool."

Not Simon. He thinks his helmet is very cool. "A helmet saved my life," he says. "Sometimes they mess up your hair, but it's worth it."

No Helmet? Pay Up! (cont.)

Directions: Answer these questions. You may look at the story.

1. What are bikers required to wear in Florida?

2. What happens if a person gets caught not wearing a helmet?

3. Describe what a person has to do so that he or she does not have to pay the ticket.

4. What could have happened to Simon Crider if he hadn't worn a helmet?

5. Explain the importance of wearing bike helmets.

6. Why do you think bike helmets only prevent head injuries 85% of the time?

7. Explain the "dork" factor.

8. What is your opinion about the use of bike helmets?

No Helmet? Pay Up! *(cont.)*

Directions: Look at the map. Answer the questions.

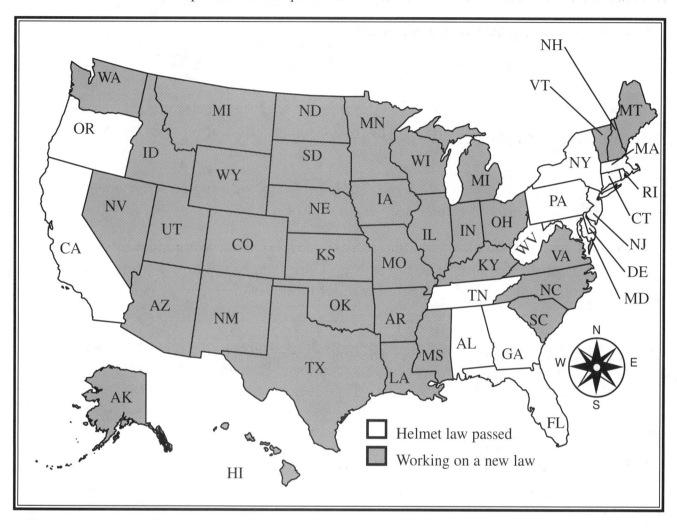

1. What is the purpose of this map of the United States?

2. What can you determine about the states that have or have not passed helmet laws?

3. Why do you think so many states have not passed helmet laws?

4. Many of the states that have passed helmet laws have high populations. Why do you think this is?

Rings Around Jupiter

Jupiter is the king of planets. It is the biggest in our solar system. There is a storm on Jupiter. It is called the Great Red Spot. You can see it with a telescope. This storm is twice as big as Earth!

Jupiter has rings. You can see Saturn's rings through a telescope, but the rings around Jupiter are very hard to see.

In 1998, scientists made a great discovery. They were studying 36 new pictures of Jupiter taken in space. They figured out how its rings are formed. Jupiter's rings are thin layers of moon dust.

Jupiter has very strong gravity. That is the force that keeps us from flying into space. Jupiter's gravity pulls comets and space rocks toward it. Some of the rocks crash into Jupiter's moons. The crash makes a big cloud of dust. The dust flies into space. Then it goes into orbit and helps form a ring.

In thousands of years, the little moons will disappear. All that will be left of them is Jupiter's dusty rings. "That could never happen to Earth's moon," says space scientist Maureen Ockert-Bell. "Our moon is just too big."

Rings Around Jupiter (cont.)

Directions: Answer these questions. You may look at the story.

1. What is the name of the storm on Jupiter?

2. What is gravity?

3. What are Jupiter's rings made of?

4. Why is Jupiter called the king of planets?

5. Why doesn't the Earth have rings?

6. Compare Jupiter to Earth. How are they similar and different?

7. How do you think scientists used pictures to determine how the rings are made?

8. Scientists say that this could never happen to Earth's moon. What does Earth's size have to do with this?

Rings Around Jupiter *(cont.)*

Directions: Look at the diagram. Answer the questions.

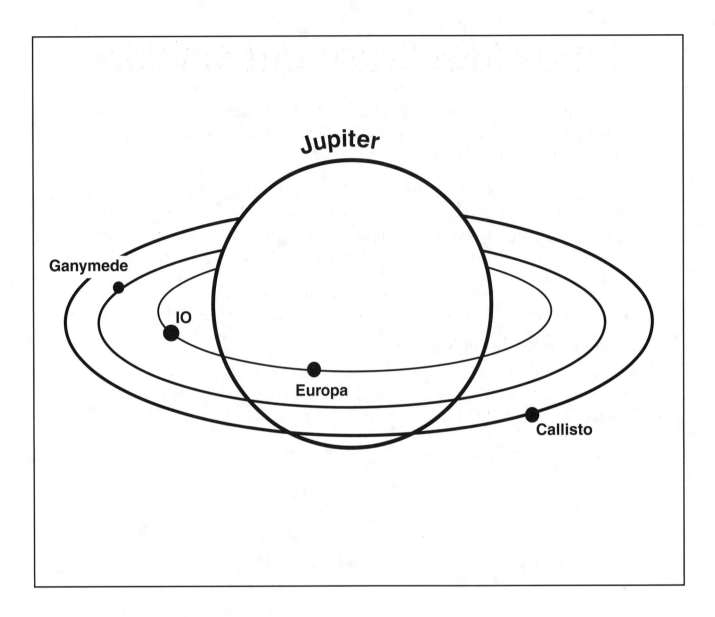

1. What do you think are the objects orbiting Jupiter?

2. Jupiter has 17 moons. In 1610, Galileo was able to see four of the moons with a telescope. Why do you think he was not able to see the other 13 moons?

Florida Kids Crush Out Smoking

What can a state get for $70 million? Florida spent it on ads against smoking. The ads were made mostly by kids. Result? The teen smoking rate made a big drop in just one year!

The teen smoking rate has gone up since the early 1990s. About three million teens smoke. In 1996, Florida won $13 billion. They got it from a lawsuit against tobacco companies. They wanted to use part of the money to stop kids from smoking. They let kids think up ideas for the ads.

It is important to keep kids from smoking. There was a study done with kids who smoke every day. It shows that these kids get lung damage. The body can never fix it.

"It didn't matter if [kids] were heavy or light smokers. What mattered was that they started young," said scientist John K. Wiencke. Thank goodness that in Florida, people who are against smoking are starting young, too!

Florida Kids Crush Out Smoking *(cont.)*

Directions: Answer these questions. You may look at the story.

1. What did Florida buy with $70 million?

2. Who were the ads made for?

3. What happens when kids smoke?

4. Why do you think some kids start smoking?

5. Part of the money was used to stop kids from smoking. What do you think the rest was used for?

6. Kids helped to think up the ads. How do you think this made the ads more effective?

7. How did the ads reduce the smoking rate?

8. Why do you think more kids started smoking in the 1990s?

Florida Kids Crush Out Smoking *(cont.)*

Directions: Read the graph. Answer the questions.

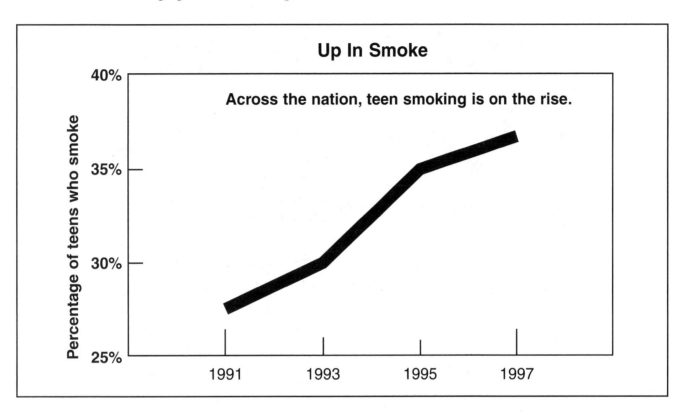

1. What is the purpose of the graph?

2. What does the graph show about the teen smoking rate in 1991 compared to 1997?

3. Why do you think the teen smoking rate is on the rise?

4. Why do you think teenagers decide to start smoking?

5. If all states were as successful as Florida in reducing teen smoking, in what direction would the graph line go in future years?

Directions: Read the story.

Antarctic Shipwreck!

When Ernest Shackleton packed for his trip in 1914, he seemed ready for anything. He and his 27-man crew filled their ship with food, tents, warm clothes, and sled dogs. The ship was called the *Endurance*. They hoped to be the first people to travel across Antarctica.

But the men did not make it. Instead, they made history in a story of survival.

The *Endurance* was just 100 miles from Antarctica when ice suddenly closed around it. It would be months before the ice melted and the ship could sail.

The ship drifted with the ice. The sailors tried to keep warm. They passed the time by playing cards. They built "dogloos" for their sled dogs.

After 10 months, the ice began to crush the ship. Shackleton ordered the men to leave the ship. The sailors were stranded on an island. So Shackleton set out to sea with five strong men. He left the others behind. They sailed and rowed 800 miles in a tiny boat.

Four months later, Shackleton returned to rescue his crew. They laughed and hugged. All 28 men of the *Endurance* trip survived. How? Perhaps because Shackleton was a true hero. As the explorer said, "If you're a leader, you've got to keep going."

Antarctic Shipwreck! *(cont.)*

Directions: Answer these questions. You may look at the story.

1. How many men were in Shackleton's crew?

2. What was their goal for the trip?

3. How can you tell that the crew was not very worried when they first got stuck?

4. How do you think the men felt when they were stranded on the island?

5. What would you do to survive on a cold, snowy island?

6. What are "dogloos"?

7. Describe what you think the trip was like for Shackleton and the five men who went for help.

8. Why do you think Shackleton was not willing to give up?

Antarctic Shipwreck! *(cont.)*

Directions: Look at the map. Answer the questions.

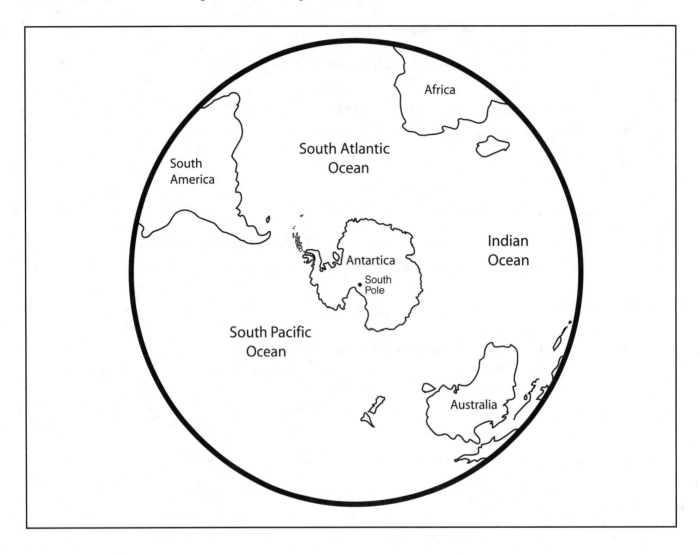

1. By looking at this map, is there a way to tell where Shackleton's crew was stranded? Why or why not?

2. In order to tell through which ocean the crew sailed to get to Antarctica, what information would you need to know first?

3. If Shackleton took the shortest route to Antarctica, from which continent would he have started his journey?

A Cereal Shake-up

The Post cereal company is about to give cereal lovers a treat. The good news is lower prices. Post said that it will cut the cost of its cereals about a dollar a box.

That's great news for shoppers. People have been complaining about the high price of cereal for years. Cereal in a box costs only about 50¢ to make. Boxes often sell for $4 or more.

The steep prices have made people wonder. More than 85% of cereal sold in the U.S. is made by four companies. Members of Congress want to find out if these companies are secretly agreeing to keep prices high. So far, no one has looked into this.

The cost of cereal includes more than just the flakes or O's you eat. The basic ingredients are similar in every box. Cereal is made of grains and sugar. So big cereal makers work hard to convince buyers that their brands are special.

These companies try to catch your eye. They create colorful boxes with cartoon characters on the front. They put games on the back. Sometimes they put prizes inside. TV ads also attempt to get your interest. Ads and fancy boxes cost money. That adds to the cereal's price.

The Post company decided to make a change. They knew that people were angry about high cereal prices. But Post isn't cutting prices just to be nice. It hopes that its lower prices will get people to buy their cereal.

A Cereal Shake-up (cont.)

Directions: Answer these questions. You may look at the story.

1. What are people angry about?

2. How much does it cost to make a box of cereal?

3. What do cereal companies do that makes the cereal more expensive?

4. Why is Post planning to lower prices?

5. How much profit is made on a box of cereal?

6. Why would all of the companies want to keep cereal prices high?

7. Why do you think people keep buying expensive cereal?

8. How do you think Post's lower prices will change cereal sales and choices?

A Cereal Shake-up (cont.)

Directions: Read the graph. Answer the questions.

The Cost of One Box

Just where does that $3.39 go when you buy an 18-ounce box of corn flakes?

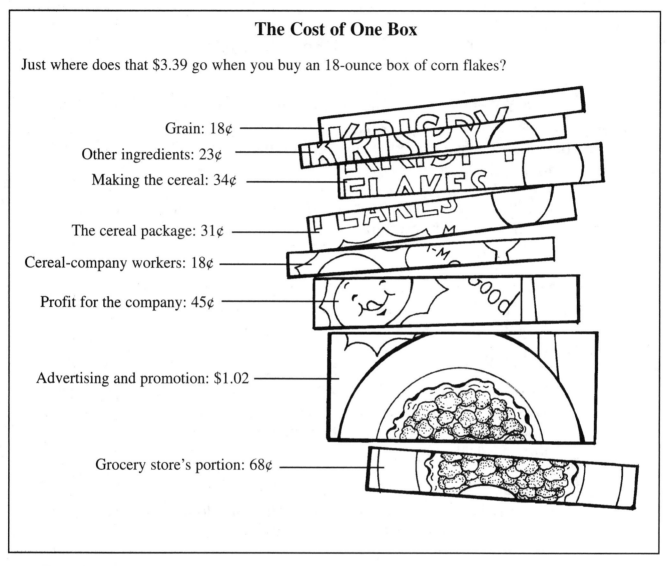

Grain: 18¢

Other ingredients: 23¢

Making the cereal: 34¢

The cereal package: 31¢

Cereal-company workers: 18¢

Profit for the company: 45¢

Advertising and promotion: $1.02

Grocery store's portion: 68¢

1. What is the purpose of this graph?

2. How much money is spent on the ingredients of the cereal?

3. The graph shows that the ingredients, cost of making the cereal, and cost of the box is only $1.06. Why does the company only make 45 cents on the sale of a box of cereal?

4. What do you think cereal companies could do to lower the cost?

Special Delivery

In 1996, there was only one librarian in Garissa. Garissa is an area of Kenya in Africa. The library had 24,000 books. Not many people came to read them. "We had to find a way to reach the people. They were not coming to us," the librarian said.

Then, he had an idea. He would take the library to the people. He knew just what to do for desert travel. The Mobile Camel Library was born!

The area is dry and sandy. Camels can go for weeks without drinking water. Their hooves are flat and wide. This is perfect for desert travel. They don't sink in the sand. Also, a camel can carry very heavy loads.

Now three camels travel twice a month. They carry boxes filled with books. Kids are happy when the library visits. In the village of Bulla Iftin, one boy said he treasures his time with each book. "I really want the book to stay in my head," he says.

What happens if someone loses a book? Library fines are pretty stiff. "If a community loses books," the librarian says, "we do not go back."

Special Delivery (cont.)

Directions: Answer these questions. You may look at the story.

1. Where is Kenya?

2. How often does the library travel?

3. Why weren't people reading the books in the library?

4. Why are camels good for desert travel?

5. How many trips does the library make in one year?

6. Why do you think the kids are happy when the library comes?

7. Describe what it's like to have a book "stay in your head."

8. Explain why you think the library stops coming to a community if they lose a book.

Special Delivery *(cont.)*

Directions: Look at the map and globe. Answer the questions.

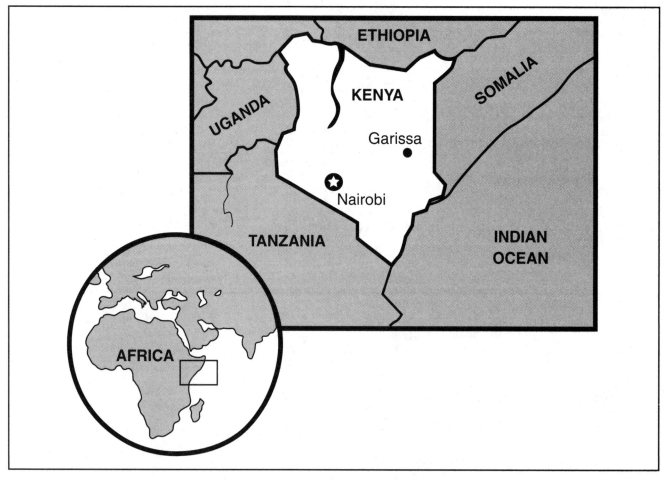

1. Why does this illustration show both the globe and a map of Kenya and the surrounding countries?

2. On what continent is Kenya?

3. What do you think the star represents on the map?

4. The Mobile Camel Library travels to many towns outside of Garissa. Why do you think these towns are not shown on the map?

Raising the Next Balto

Rohn and Nikolai may have the world's best job. The brothers work at the Happy Trails Kennel in Alaska. They help train 20 puppies a year.

"We don't have to do it. We like to," says Nikolai. The puppies grow up to run in the Iditarod. This is a yearly dogsled race from Anchorage to Nome, Alaska. The race on March 1 follows an old path. Dog teams raced on this path to bring medicine to sick kids.

Their dad is Martin Buser. He is a professional dogsled racer. He has won the Iditarod twice. He even named Rohn and Nikolai after stops on the trail. Buser wants the puppies at his kennel to have plenty of love. He knows the human touch will make them better sled dogs.

While the pups are tiny, the boys pet and cuddle them a lot. "That's what makes them really used to people," says Rohn. He and his brother watch videos with snoozing puppies tucked inside their shirts.

Nikolai and Rohn run around with the puppies for hours every day. Race dogs need to have their feet checked for injuries during races. The boys rub each dog's feet to get it used to having them checked. They go out on training runs with the dogs. They tie a small doglsed behind their dad's full-size one. The puppies start training with a sled when they're about 9 months old.

Which pup is the very best? "We don't really have favorite puppies," says Nikolai. "We like them all."

Raising the Next Balto *(cont.)*

Directions: Answer these questions. You may look at the story.

1. What job do Rohn and Nikolai have?

2. What will the puppies do when they grow up?

3. What makes them better sled dogs?

4. Explain several things the boys do with the puppies.

5. How many puppies would they train in five years?

6. Why do the puppies need to be comfortable with having their feet touched?

7. Explain why this job is considered to be so great.

8. What do you think about dogs running in sled races?

Raising the Next Balto *(cont.)*

Directions: Look at the map. Answer the questions.

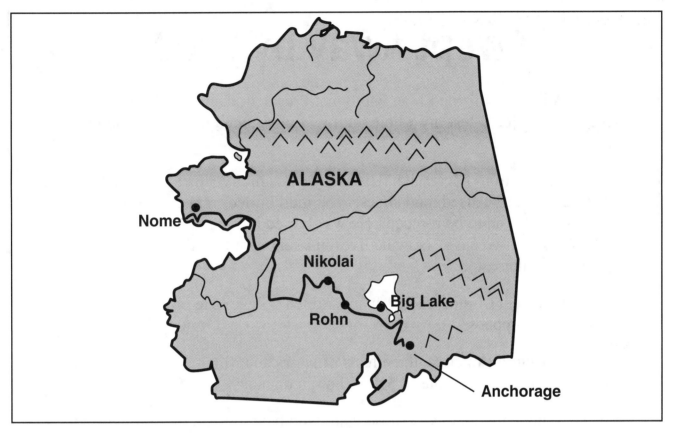

1. What does this map show?

2. How is this map helpful in better understanding the article?

3. Notice the jagged path of the Iditarod trail. Why do you think it doesn't go in a straight line?

4. Notice the areas of mountains on the map. What does this tell you about the Iditarod race?

5. Why do you think Martin Buser named his sons after two stops on the Iditarod trail?

Swept Away by Mitch

A little boy named Juan Pablo met President Clinton. He spoke softly. He said, "I lost my whole family. I miss them, my mama and my papa."

Juan is from Nicaragua. His village was hit by Hurricane Mitch. The heavy rains caused mud slides. The mud buried farms. It buried homes. Juan had to be rescued. He was buried in mud up to his neck. He was stuck for two days. Now he lives in a tent camp. A thousand other people live there, too.

President Clinton visited Juan's ruined village. He brought some money and supplies.

In Central America, the effects of Hurricane Mitch are still felt. The storm killed 9,000. It caused $10 billion in damage.

Many children died. Those who lived have found it hard to return to normal life. Homeless teenagers are drifting north toward Mexico. They are looking for work and a place to live. Many kids are out of school. That's because the buildings are being used as emergency housing.

The U.S. and other countries have sent some money to help Central America. The area needs even more help. The president has asked Congress for $956 million more. Congress has not yet approved it. While Congress is deciding, people are dying. We need to help one another. We need to help the people in Nicaragua.

Swept Away by Mitch (cont.)

Directions: Answer these questions. You may look at the story.

1. What is Mitch?

2. What did Mitch cause?

3. What happened to Juan Pablo?

4. Why do the people live in camps now?

5. The storm killed 9,000 people. If there were five people in each family, how many families were killed by the storm?

6. How do you think Juan Pablo was able to survive for two days in the mud?

7. What do you think would need to be done to repair a town destroyed by rain and mudslides?

8. What is the message of this article?

Swept Away by Mitch *(cont.)*

Directions: Look at the map and globe. Answer the questions.

The Effects of Hurricane Mitch

1. Nicaragua is located between what two large continents?

2. Why do you think that some of the countries on the map are shaded?

3. Hurricanes begin over the ocean. What does the map show about how much Nicaragua could be effected by hurricanes?

4. How does the map help you to better understand the article?

Directions: Read the story.

Do Girls Know Best?

Have you ever laughed so hard that it made you snort? Forgotten to zip up your pants all the way? Zoya Ahmadi feels your pain. She says, "I know being embarrassed in public is one of the worst things girls have to face." She doesn't bury her face after slip-ups like those. Instead, she wrote a chapter of advice. It is to help other girls avoid embarrassing moments.

Zoya's chapter is one of 26 in a new book called *Girls Know Best*. All the chapters are written by girls, ages 7 to 16. They were chosen through a writing contest. The editor says that the book "encourages girls to speak out and be heard. It's a way for them to talk to each other."

Girls across the country had a lot to say. Two sisters wrote about surviving sibling fights. Two friends wrote a chapter called "BIG Words to Use to Impress Friends, Parents, and Teachers."

The book has 38 authors. They have visited stores around the country. They autograph books for people. Another *Girls Know Best* book is already in the works. And for boys who think they know best, your turn is coming. A boys-only book is on the way.

Directions: Answer these questions. You may look at the story.

1. What does Zoya say is the worst thing?

2. What did Zoya write?

3. How were the book's authors chosen?

4. If half of the chapters had one author and half had two authors, how many authors would have contributed to the book?

5. How would this book be helpful to girls?

6. Why do you think the book is called *Girls Know Best*?

7. If you could write a chapter of an advice book, what would you write about?

8. What kinds of topics do you think would be included in a book called *Boys Know Best*?

Do Girls Know Best? *(cont.)*

Directions: Read the Table of Contents. Answer the questions.

Table of Contents

Cats Know Best

1. On what page would you find information about grooming?

2. Which chapter in this book is the longest?

3. Which chapter would tell about cats hunting for birds?

Directions: Read the story.

Marathon Madness

What makes 15,000 men and women take off their jackets on a chilly day in April and run for four hours or more through the streets of Greater Boston? Put like that, it certainly sounds silly, but I was one of those runners. In fact, like everybody else, I even paid for the experience.

The race is called the Boston Marathon, and people have been competing in it since 1897.

"I could do that," I said.

"No, you couldn't," my friend Ed replied.

"Want to bet?" I said. And that's how it happened.

There were times when I regretted the dare. I had never run more than eight miles at a stretch before, and here I was training for over three times that distance. To make matters worse, since the race is in April, I had to run throughout the winter, and in Boston winters are cold. For most people just putting on their shirts, sweaters, jackets, mittens, and hats is exercise enough. I found myself out on the dark January streets, jumping over snow banks and skidding along icy patches of sidewalk. Even in gloves my fingers got so cold that they felt like rolls of pennies; my nose didn't defrost until lunchtime!

Finally, the big day arrived. The weather was cold with ice and rain.

Bang! A gun sounded, and we were off. Well, I didn't actually go anywhere at first because I was standing behind so many people, and I had to wait for them to move. It was like being in a traffic jam, so I just jumped up and down to stay warm.

At first, the running was easy. The other runners just seemed to pull me along. Somewhere around the 20-mile mark I even caught myself thinking, "This is nothing. Why did I train so hard?"

That's when I hit "the wall." I didn't actually run into a brick wall, but it felt as if I had. "The wall" is what marathoners call the point at which a body simply runs out of gas. My legs turned to rubber; my arms turned into pieces of wood. I thought I might pass out. I can't remember anything about the last five miles of the race.

I kept running though. At least, that's what Ed told me at the finish line.

"You looked good," he said. "How did it feel?"

"Terrific," I lied. I wasn't going to let him get the last laugh.

Marathon Madness (cont.)

Directions: Answer these questions. You may look at the story.

1. How many people were in the marathon?

2. Why did the author decide to participate in the marathon?

3. What is a marathon?

4. What is involved in training for a marathon?

5. Why didn't everyone move right when the gun went off?

6. Why did the author say his fingers felt like rolls of pennies?

7. How do you think his body felt when he hit "the wall"?

8. Why would a person decide to run such a long, painful race?

Marathon Madness *(cont.)*

Directions: Look at the map. Answer the questions.

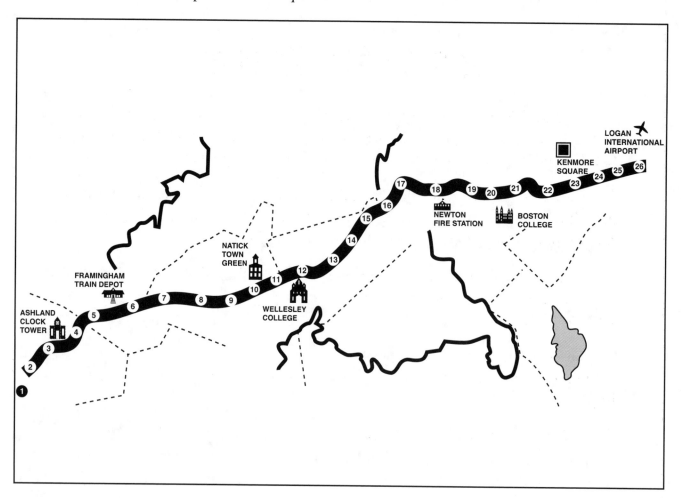

1. What does this map show?

2. Is the race run in a city or in the countryside? How can you tell?

3. How many miles long is the marathon?

Directions: Read the story.

It's Outta There!

Mark McGwire bent over home plate. The bat looked tiny in his big hands. Then he swung with all his might. The ball flew 458 feet over the fence. The crowd roared with joy. It was his 59th home run of the season.

McGwire played for the St. Louis Cardinals. He and Sammy Sosa of the Chicago Cubs made it one hot summer for homers that year. Both McGwire and Sosa hoped to break a baseball record.

In 1961, New York Yankee Roger Maris broke Babe Ruth's record of 60 home runs in a season. Maris hit 61. For 37 years, folks have wondered who would break Maris' record.

McGwire looked like a sure bet. But Sosa was right behind him. "Quite amazing, isn't it?" said McGwire. "What's going on now is pretty big!"

Fans sure thought so. Thousands turned up just to watch McGwire practice batting. No one rooted harder for him than his son. He often got to be the bat boy for his dad's team.

His son was also the first one to meet him at home plate when he hit number 62, breaking Maris' record. McGwire went on to set a new record with 70 home runs for the 1998 season!

It's Outta There! (cont.)

Directions: Answer these questions. You may look at the story.

1. Who is Mark McGwire?

2. What did McGwire and Sosa want to do?

3. Whose record were they trying to beat?

4. Do you think players break home run records every year? Why?

5. What do you think the players did to be able to hit so many home runs?

6. Why did so many people come to watch McGwire?

7. Why did the author think McGwire would break the record?

8. How do you think the author feels about the 1998 baseball season?

It's Outta There! *(cont.)*

Directions: Look at the graph. Answer the questions.

Sluggers McGwire, Sosa, and Griffey were all trying to break Maris' record for the most home runs in a season. This graph shows how many homers each player hit each month through August 1998. (Each player's final total when the season ended was higher.)

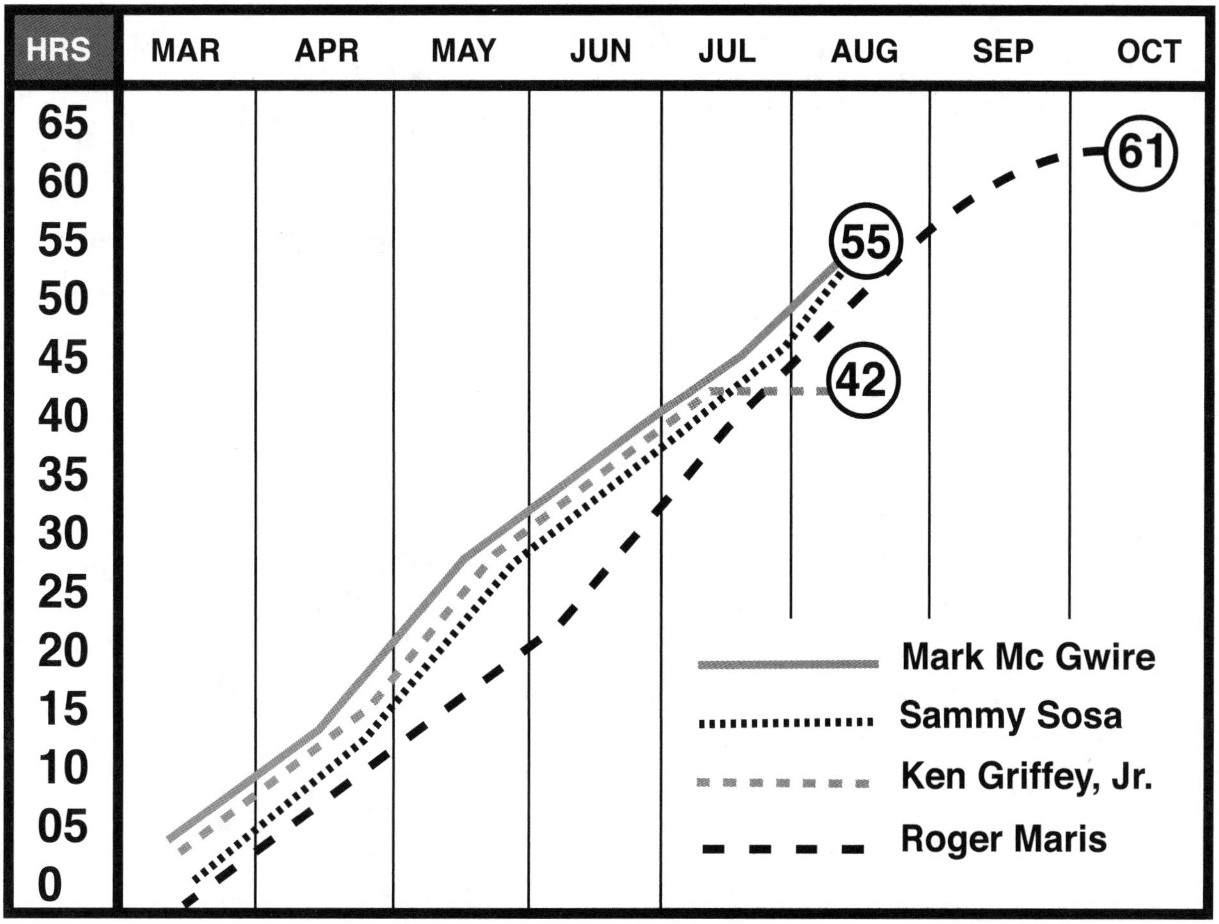

HRS	MAR	APR	MAY	JUN	JUL	AUG	SEP	OCT

(Graph showing home run totals by month)

Values marked on graph: 65, 60, 55, 50, 45, 40, 35, 30, 25, 20, 15, 10, 05, 0

Circled values on graph: 61 (OCT), 55 (AUG), 42 (AUG)

Legend:
— Mark Mc Gwire
·········· Sammy Sosa
- - - Ken Griffey, Jr.
– – – Roger Maris

1. How does this graph relate to the article?

2. Why are there only four baseball players represented on the graph?

3. Why are the lines of the graph made with different patterns?

4. What does the graph show about the home run totals of McGwire and Sosa in August?

Winds of Destruction

The howling winds and sheets of rain came first. Palm trees were pounded by wind and rain. They bent over and touched the ground. Roofs lifted off buildings. Water flooded roads. Huge waves sent boats crashing into one another.

Next came the calm weather. The sun was bright and the skies were clear and blue. The damage could be seen. Electric-power lines, trees, and pieces of homes were scattered everywhere.

This scene was played over and over again. It was Hurricane Georges. It roared through the islands of the Caribbean. Then it headed to Florida. The hurricane destroyed everything in its path.

Not an inch of Puerto Rico was spared from the storm. Its 110-mile-an-hour winds ripped up power lines and roofs. "This thing was a monster," said Pedro Juan Morales. His home was badly damaged. But he was luckier than most. The storm left many houses without electricity or running water. Many people were homeless.

The storm lashed into Florida. People were told to leave their homes. They needed to find shelter. One woman said, "When I return, I may not have a home."

Georges was blamed for billions of dollars worth of damage. Worse, it also killed more than 300 people.

Winds of Destruction (cont.)

Directions: Answer these questions. You may look at the story.

1. What places did the hurricane hit?

2. How much did the damage cost?

3. What is a hurricane?

4. What can a hurricane do?

5. What do you think could be done to protect a home from a hurricane?

6. Why did people have to leave their homes?

7. Why was Pedro Juan Morales lucky?

8. Summarize the article using three sentences.

Winds of Destruction *(cont.)*

Directions: Look at the diagram. Answer the questions.

Caribbean hurricanes form when high storm clouds move over warm tropical waters. Fed by warm water and hot air, a column–the eye–forms in the center. Winds spin counterclockwise around the eye. When the winds reach a speed of 74 miles an hour, the storm is called a hurricane. Storms pick up speed over water and weaken when they hit land.

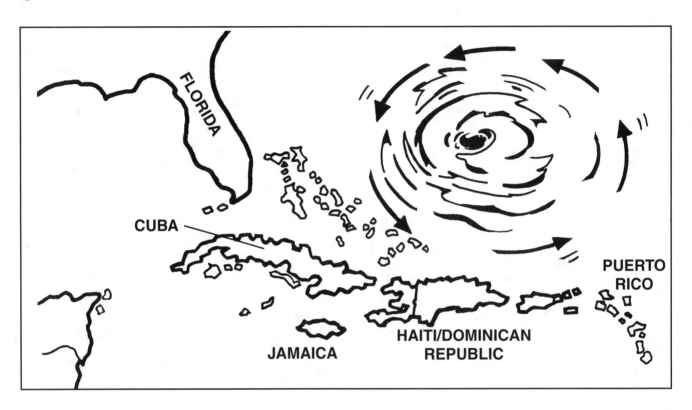

1. What does it mean that the hurricane spins counterclockwise?

2. In the illustration above, where is the eye of the hurricane. Draw an X on it.

3. Hurricanes weaken when they hit land. If this hurricane is headed toward Florida, when do you think it will stop?

     ©*Teacher Created Materials, Inc.*

A Safety Net for Salmon

Pacific salmon have a wonderful childhood. They wiggle around in cool creeks. They swim with their brothers and sisters. When they are bigger, they head for the ocean. That's where they grow up.

But after a few years, life gets tough for salmon. Something in their nature tells them to go home. They push their way upstream. They go back to where they were born. Some travel hundreds of miles! They swim and jump against the currents that once carried them out to sea. Once there, they lay eggs and then die.

It's a hard life. But some people have made it even harder. Too much fishing and pollution have killed too many salmon. Much of their habitat has been destroyed.

Last week it was announced that seven kinds of salmon will be protected.

There's no way to keep people away from the river systems in Washington and Oregon, where the salmon swim. At least 5 million people live near these waterways. The big cities of Portland and Seattle are nearby.

Protecting salmon will change the way people farm, fish, and harvest wood. It will change how they build homes, use water and chemicals, and work. All those things can affect the salmon rivers. Some of the fish-saving plans may cost a lot of money. But people say they are willing to do it.

Local leaders are making plans to follow the new rules. Some groups are already taking steps to help the salmon.

After all, both people and salmon need the same things. They need clean water, shady trees, and a safe place to call home.

A Safety Net for Salmon *(cont.)*

Directions: Answer these questions. You may look at the story.

1. Where do salmon go to grow up?

2. Where do they go after a few years?

3. What is wonderful about a salmon's childhood?

4. Why do some salmon travel hundreds of miles?

5. What makes it hard for salmon to get home?

6. What should be done to protect the habitat of salmon?

7. How are salmon similar to people?

8. Why do you think people are willing to spend so much money to save them?

     ©*Teacher Created Materials, Inc.*

A Safety Net for Salmon *(cont.)*

Directions: Look at the life cycle. Answer the questions.

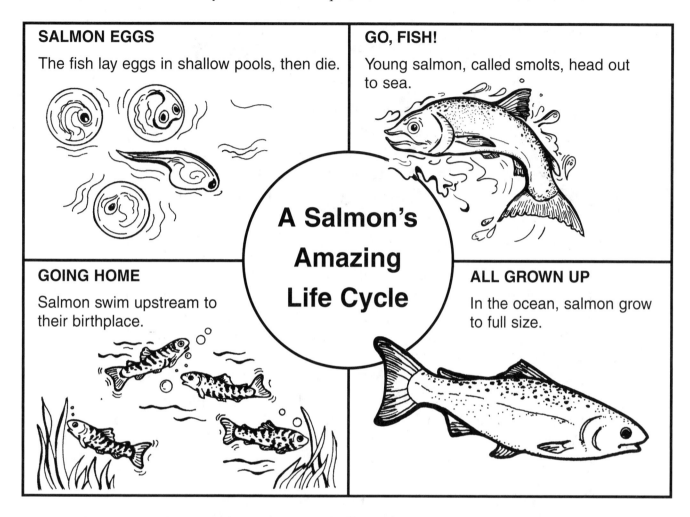

SALMON EGGS

The fish lay eggs in shallow pools, then die.

GO, FISH!

Young salmon, called smolts, head out to sea.

A Salmon's Amazing Life Cycle

GOING HOME

Salmon swim upstream to their birthplace.

ALL GROWN UP

In the ocean, salmon grow to full size.

1. What does this diagram show?

2. Why do you think the author included this diagram in the article?

3. Why do you think the diagram shows the stages of a salmon's life in a circular pattern?

4. Why is there no beginning point shown on the diagram?

Food for Thought

It's time to stop kidding ourselves. Freedom of choice is not always a good thing. Sure, it's great to be able to choose a movie. Who wants to be told what to watch? And it's fun to choose what clothes to wear to school or what station you listen to on the radio. But there are some things that are just too important. I'm talking about our new school cafeteria with its choice between fast-food and regular food.

Cafeteria food was never very good. Okay, sometimes it was pretty terrible. But there was always an attempt to offer a balanced diet. You'd get a plate with something brown and something green and something white on it. Somebody out there was trying to make us eat our vegetables. A lot of us didn't like it, so we brought our own lunches instead.

How do you make kids eat cafeteria food? There are two ways. The school chose the wrong one. First, you can improve the quality of the food. You can make it healthy, tasty, and fresh. Second, you can serve food you know kids will eat. Open up a burger and fries joint so that students can buy McLunch.

That's exactly what happened at our school. A week after the new fast-food counter opened, two-thirds of the students said they were ordering fries and shakes for lunch. There was quite a wait. If you wanted to get your food fast, you had to go to the old counter.

This is a choice, but it is not a healthy choice. This is a country where half the people are overweight. A school is not doing its duty by allowing students to eat a lot of fat for lunch. This school should be in the business of education. It should teach in the cafeteria as well as in the classroom. We should be learning about healthy food. We should learn about good eating habits. Above all, we should be learning that good food does not have to taste bad.

Food for Thought (cont.)

Directions: Answer these questions. You may look at the story.

1. What choice does the author say is not good?

2. What kind of food did the school start serving?

3. What did kids start ordering for lunch?

4. Why is fast food unhealthy?

5. Describe a healthy meal for lunch.

6. Why is choice sometimes not a good thing?

7. How can a school cafeteria educate kids?

8. What do you think about the author's opinion?

Food for Thought *(cont.)*

Directions: Look at the Food Guide Pyramid. Answer the questions.

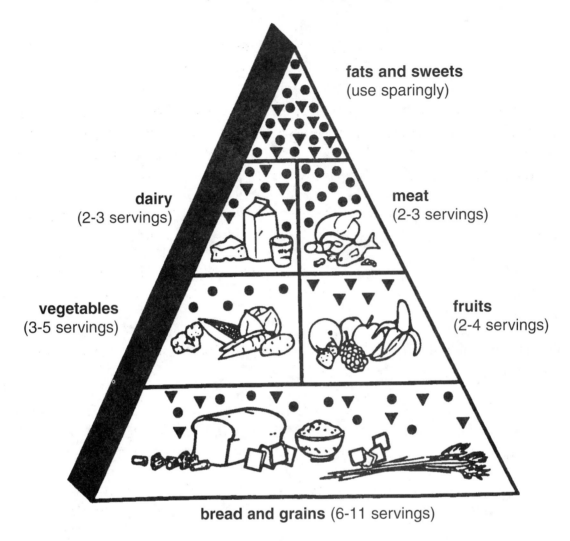

fats and sweets
(use sparingly)

dairy
(2-3 servings)

meat
(2-3 servings)

vegetables
(3-5 servings)

fruits
(2-4 servings)

bread and grains (6-11 servings)

1. Think about a fast-food meal of a hamburger, fries, and a milk shake. What food categories are represented in this meal?

2. What food categories are missing from this meal?

3. Plan a healthy lunch using the Food Guide Pyramid.

The Big Chill

How cold was it in Alaska in February 1999? Well, when Ben Dallin threw a panful of boiling water into the air, it never came back down. "It just froze into fog and made a really cool sound," says Ben. In Ben's town of McGrath, it was 62 degrees below zero!

For two weeks, an icy chill covered Alaska. Temperatures dropped as low as –77 degrees. High winds make it feel even colder.

Alaskans are used to bad weather. Schools hardly ever close due to the cold. Only when the temperature dips to –20 degrees are students excused from outdoor recess.

But extreme cold causes problems. "It's hard to talk because your lips kind of go numb," says Abbe Skinner.

Machines can go numb, too. Planes can't take off. The fuel thickens up in the cold. Heating oil gets gunky. It's hard to make stoves work. Cars won't start, so people bring car batteries inside for the night.

Snow turns powdery and dry in such cold. Walking on it makes a weird squeaking noise. "It sounds like Styrofoam," says Arianna Solie.

Wood, plastic, and even metal snap as the temperature plummets. Trees crack and fall over. Pipes burst when water freezes inside them. One boy tried to start a snowmobile and the key broke off!

Becky Campbell thinks it's a good idea to go outside even in the coldest weather. "It's nice to be outside," she says. "It's part of Alaska. I don't let it get in my way."

The Big Chill (cont.)

Directions: Answer these questions. You may look at the story.

1. What happened to the water Ben threw into the air?

2. What was the temperature that day?

3. Why aren't Alaskans bothered by cold weather?

4. What happens to fuel in cold weather?

5. Why do people bring their car batteries in for the night?

6. Think about the things you keep in your yard or on the patio. What things would be damaged by the cold?

7. How do you think people prepare for the freezing cold months?

8. Summarize the story using three sentences.

The Big Chill *(cont.)*

Average Temperatures in Alaska in January

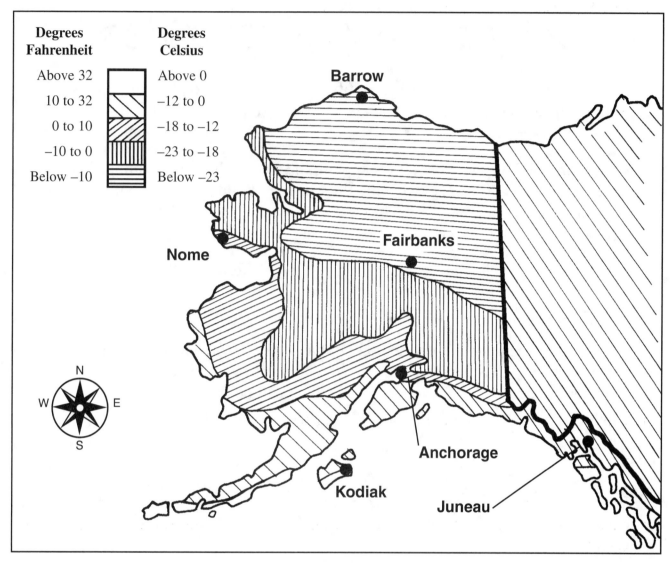

Alaska

1. Much of Alaska's coast has the warmest weather in January. Why do you think this is?

2. Which two cities have the coldest temperatures?

3. In what area of Alaska do you think Ben lives?

China's Dam Is a Good Idea

China's Yangtze River is beautiful. But the river floods. The floods have killed many people. Now a new dam will stop these floods. It will also create electricity.

In 1997, China took a big step with the river. The people dumped rocks into parts of it. They were getting ready to build a dam. It will be finished in 2009. It will be the biggest in the world. It will stop the flooding. It will turn the water's energy into electricity.

Some people don't want the dam. A long lake will be formed by it. It will swallow up villages. Millions of people must move. The dam will ruin the homes of giant pandas, river dolphins, and other rare animals.

Still, the dam will do more good than harm. More electricity will help make new businesses. The people who must move are the ones put in danger by the floods. Some wildlife habitats will be destroyed, but many more will stay. Progress often causes problems. The Three Gorges Dam is a great example of progress!

China's Dam Is a Good Idea (cont.)

Directions: Answer these questions. You may look at the story.

1. What is the problem with the Yangtze River?

2. What will stop the flooding?

3. For what will the water in the dam be used?

4. Why don't some people want the dam?

5. Who will benefit from the dam's electricity?

6. What is progress?

7. How will the dam be helpful?

8. How might the dam change the environment in a bad way?

China's Dam Is a Good Idea (cont.)

Directions: Look at the map. Answer the questions.

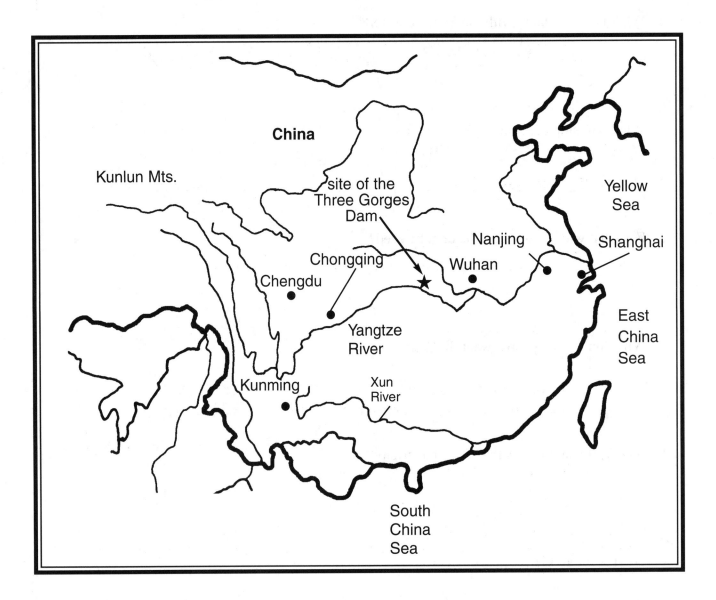

1. What is the purpose of this map?

2. Which cites do you think will be most affected by the dam?

The Wolf Packs Are Back

For hundreds of years, wolves roamed the West. But when white settlers came in the 1800s, they feared them. Wolves often killed sheep and cattle.

To help farmers, the government paid to kill wolves. By the early 1930s, all of the wolves in Yellowstone National Park were gone.

Killing the wolves had a big effect on the animals and plants. Coyotes and elk are hunted by wolves. With the wolves gone, these animals grew in numbers. Plants that are eaten by elk began to disappear. The government decided to bring wolves back to Yellowstone. It trapped some in Canada. The wolves were moved to the park. The goal is to put nature back into balance.

Not everyone was glad to see the wolves return. Farmers near the park were angry. The wolves have killed some sheep and cattle.

Some people think returning the wolves was against the law. A judge agreed with them. The judge said the wolves should be removed.

Many experts are fighting the judge's decision. The wolves have helped the park. Native plants are growing because there are fewer elk eating them. Beavers, which eat these plants, are also helped. Animals from the grizzly bear to the carrion beetle are doing well.

The wolves have a good friend named Bruce Babbitt. He is in charge of national parks. Babbitt says, "I will fight with everything I have to keep the wolves in Yellowstone." Anyone who cares about wildlife should join this fight.

The Wolf Packs Are Back (cont.)

Directions: Answer these questions. You may look at the story.

1. What did the wolves hunt?

2. Who paid to have wolves killed?

3. What happened to the elk when the wolves were gone?

4. How did the farmers feel when the wolves came back?

5. How does a national park help animals?

6. What does it mean when nature is out of balance?

7. Why is Babbitt a friend to wolves?

8. What is the main message of this story?

     ©*Teacher Created Materials, Inc.*

The Wolf Packs Are Back (cont.)

Directions: Look at the maps. Answer the questions.

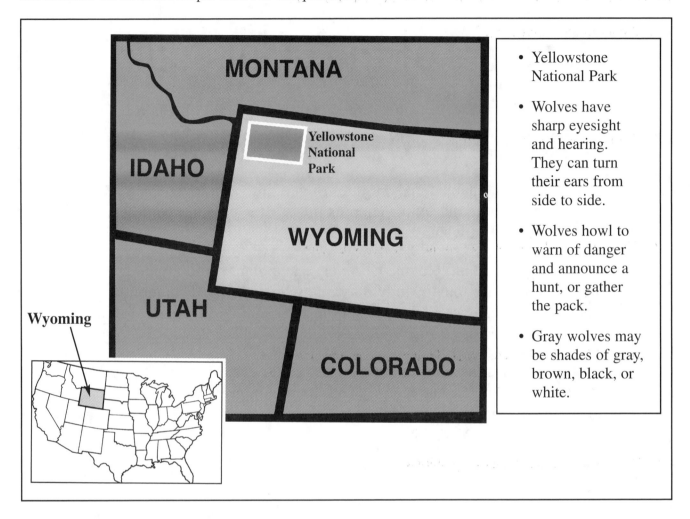

1. Why does this illustration include two overlapping maps?

2. If there are wolves in Yellowstone Park, what other states probably have wolves, also?

3. If wolves can be gray, brown, black, or white, why do you think they are all called gray wolves?

Directions: Read the story.

Secrets of the Giant Squid

It lies still and wet in a giant metal tank wrapped with chains. The case is too big to fit through any of the doors in New York City's American Museum of Natural History. On the case are the letters S-Q-U-I-D-Z-I-L-L-A.

"We keep it chained up so it doesn't get out," jokes Neil Landman. He's a scientist at the museum. There is no way the creature could get out — it's dead. But what exactly is it?

It's a giant squid. No one has ever seen a giant squid alive. Scientists have been able to study only a few body parts. This month, museum visitors can get a look at the monster. Squidzilla will be displayed in a huge plastic case.

Squidzilla is the most complete giant squid ever studied. It has all eight of its arms and two tentacles! The squid is in great shape. When the dead squid landed in a fisherman's net, he froze it so it wouldn't rot. Then it was flown to New York City.

Squidzilla is 25 feet long and weighs 200 pounds. At first, the scientists thought they had a baby giant squid. Its arm are much shorter than others they had seen. Scientists think giant squid can be as much as 60 feet long and weigh more than a ton.

After studying it, the scientists decided it is a full-grown male. They think females have longer arms. Giant squid swim in deep waters. Scientists aren't sure how many giant squid there are. They don't even know where they live. Don't hold your breath waiting for answers. As long as they stay deep in the ocean's dark waters, giant squid will probably remain a mystery.

Secrets of the Giant Squid *(cont.)*

Directions: Answer these questions. You may look at the story.

1. Who found the squid?

2. Why is it in such good condition?

3. Why couldn't the squid get out of the tank?

4. The giant squid weighs 200 pounds. Name something else that weighs about this much.

5. How is this squid different from others scientists have found?

6. Why do scientists think the squid is a male?

7. Why don't scientists know much about giant squid?

8. How do you think the scientists felt about this discovery? Why?

Secrets of the Giant Squid *(cont.)*

Directions: Look at the diagram. Answer the questions.

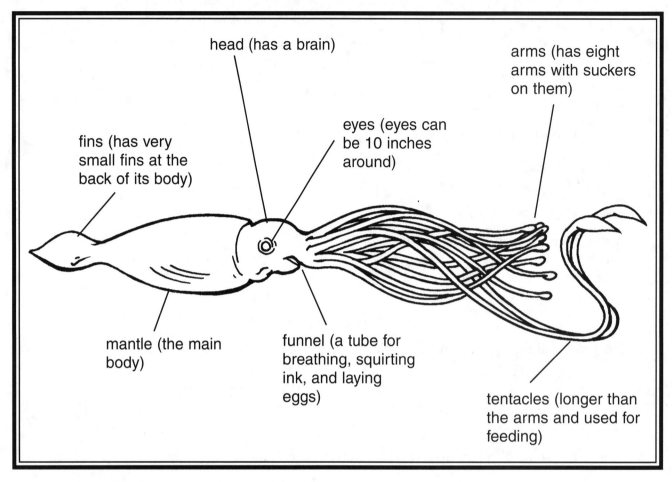

head (has a brain)

arms (has eight arms with suckers on them)

eyes (eyes can be 10 inches around)

fins (has very small fins at the back of its body)

mantle (the main body)

funnel (a tube for breathing, squirting ink, and laying eggs)

tentacles (longer than the arms and used for feeding)

1. Compare the body of a squid to the body of a typical fish. Write how they are the same and different.

2. How do you think the squid's arms are used for feeding?

3. Why do you think scientists are so interested in the giant squid?

4. How could a teacher use a diagram of a squid to teach students?

5. What does the diagram teach you about the squid that the article does not?

The Next Wave of Energy

Think of all the ways you used electricity today. Did you turn on a light this morning? Did you listen to the radio? Did you watch TV? All these things use electric power.

Where does this power come from? In most places in the world, it comes from burning fuels. These fuels are gas, coal, and oil. Big factories called power plants burn these fuels. It makes electricity.

Gas, coal, and oil are called fossil fuels. They are formed deep in the earth. This happens from the breakdown of animals and plants that lived millions of years ago. It takes that long for fossil fuels to form.

Fossil fuels have been the world's main source of energy for a long time. But burning them gives off dirty gases. This is the main cause of pollution. Scientists have been looking for cleaner ways to light our lamps and heat our homes. They've found answers. They are blowing in the wind and shining in sunlight.

On April 22, people take time to think about the environment. This is called Earth Day. In some cities, Earth Day is every day. They use the sun and the wind for energy.

Using the power of the sun can be tricky. Scientists are still trying to figure out the best ways to catch sunlight and turn it into electricity.

In Japan, companies are making a special type of house. It has special roof tiles to absorb sunshine. The tiles work very well. They can make enough electricity for an entire family! And they are not too expensive to make. About 70,000 of these homes will be built in the next few years.

Windmills are also a source of energy. They have been used for hundreds of years. Modern windmills have lightweight blades that can catch more wind than ever before. "Windmills are taking an old technology and making it work today," says Jim Marston.

New windmills are popping up all over the U.S., Europe, and Asia. Denmark gets 6% of its electricity from wind power.

Our supply of fossil fuels is limited. But the energy we can get from the sun and the wind is endless!

The Next Wave of Energy *(cont.)*

Directions: Answer these questions. You may look at the story.

1. What are three fuels that are burned to make power?

2. What are fossil fuels?

3. What are two other sources of energy?

4. How can you help to take care of the environment?

5. The article says that answers are blowing in the wind and shining in the sun. What does that mean?

6. Why is it better to use power from the sun and wind?

7. If you could plan your own town, what three things would you do to help the environment?

8. Write three reasons to support the use of power from the wind and sun.

The Next Wave of Energy *(cont.)*

Directions: Look at the idea web. Answer the questions.

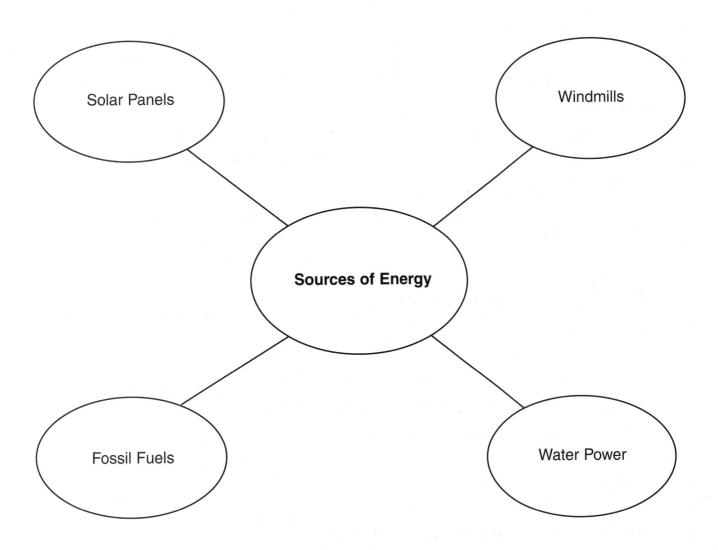

1. Which of the energy sources on the web is not discussed in the article?

2. How could an idea web like this one be useful to you in writing a summary of the article?

Save Our Streams

Have you ever been boating on a river? You would expect to see clear water, fish, birds, and healthy plants. Let me tell you about my trip down our local river.

I saw a refrigerator, a dead cow, and soda pop cans. I saw plastic cups, sewer pipes, and dirty water. I didn't enjoy this trip. There was too much pollution in the river.

I feel the president should make cleaning up our waterways one of the first things he does. He should do this because we drink water from this river and other rivers like it. We need water. We need it to be clean. We can get sick from dirty water and die!

I would like to see our rivers cleaned up. This would give us clean drinking water and a great place to fish. This could be done by removing the trash and waste products. Then we would make sure that they do not get put back into the river. Maybe our laws could be more strict. People would think before they polluted our rivers.

When I grow up, I want to bring my son down the river. I want him to see only fish, birds, clean water, and green plants. Wouldn't it be nice if he could also take a drink?

Sincerely,

Matthew Raborn, 10
Our Lady of Fatima School
Lafayette, Louisiana

Save Our Streams (cont.)

Directions: Answer these questions. You may look at the story.

1. Why is the author unhappy?

2. What does he want the president to do?

3. What did the boy see in the water?

4. What does the word *local* mean?

5. What can you do to help keep waterways clean?

6. Pretend that you are a lawmaker. Write a law about keeping rivers clean.

7. In your opinion, who should help to keep waterways clean?

8. What is the purpose of this letter?

Save Our Streams *(cont.)*

Directions: Read the outline. Answer the questions.

I. I went on a river trip.

    A. The river was polluted.

        1. I saw a refrigerator, a dead cow, soda cans, plastic cups, and sewer pipes.

        2. The water was dirty.

II. The president should take care of this problem.

    A. We need clean water.

        1. Dirty water could make people sick.

        2. Dirty water could kill people.

    B. People need to clean up.

        1. Trash and waste should be removed.

        2. There should be strict laws.

III. I want my own son to be able to enjoy the river.

1. How does an outline help a person when writing a letter or a story?

2. What other things could the author have mentioned in his letter?

Keiko Goes Home

Keiko's journey began in the cold blue waters of the Atlantic Ocean. He was born about 20 years ago. At age 2, he was captured. He was taken to an aquarium in Iceland. He would never swim with his pod again.

Soon after that, he was moved to another aquarium in Canada. He began performing tricks for people. But he made his big splash when an aquarium in Mexico bought him. That's where he landed the lead whale role in *Free Willy*. The movie made Keiko a star.

In the movie, Keiko's character lives in a theme park. He suffers through awful living conditions. In real life, Keiko's life wasn't much better. His pool in Mexico was too small. It was also too warm. His skin was once glossy and slick. Then it broke out in sores. The big fin on his back flopped sadly over to one side.

Keiko's fans rushed to help. They formed a group called the Free Willy Keiko Foundation. They raised enough money to fly him to a pool in Newport, Oregon. In his cool new pool, Keiko's health improved right away. His skin sores went away. He gained 2,000 pounds. Soon he was strong enough for a trip home.

Keiko was getting stronger. His caretakers were busy making a new home for him in Iceland. Keiko couldn't be set free. He had lived almost his whole life in captivity. It was too risky just to set him free. The solution was to build a giant floating pen in the north Atlantic Ocean. The pen is 250 feet long. It has walls made of special nets so that fish swim in and out. Keiko can see and hear nearby whales and birds.

Keiko Goes Home (cont.)

Directions: Answer these questions. You may look at the story.

1. Where was Keiko born?

2. Why doesn't he still live there?

3. How was Keiko's life like the movie *Free Willy*?

4. Compare Keiko's condition to a healthy whale.

5. How did Keiko's life improve?

6. What would you include in the ideal aquarium for Keiko?

7. What was a sign that Keiko was getting stronger?

8. What would you recommend to help Keiko in the future?

Keiko Goes Home *(cont.)*

Directions: Look at the map. Answer the questions.

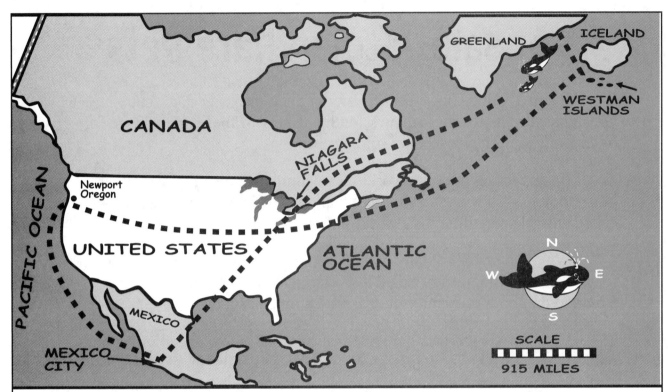

A WHALE OF A TRAIL Keiko's journey began in the Atlantic Ocean near Iceland. In 1982, he was taken to a marine animal park in Canada. Then he went to Mexico and in 1996 to Oregon. Last stop: back to Iceland!

1. How does this map add to the article about Keiko?

2. The map shows Keiko's path going over land. How do you think Keiko was able to travel out of the water?

3. What is different about the compass on this map?

4. When Keiko was in Mexico City, about how many miles was he away from home?

For Sale: Stolen Rare Pets

It's in Mexico City. Animals are jammed into cages at a market. Green parrots and toucans squawk loudly. Many of these animals are rare or endangered. They are being sold as pets.

It happens all over the world. Rare animals are stolen from their jungle homes. They are taken to pet markets. This is illegal business. It is called animal smuggling. It's worth billions of dollars a year.

Why is it so big? Many people want rare pets. They will pay $3,000 for a bird from Brazil. It's called a scarlet macaw. A lizard called the Komodo dragon is very rare. It sells for as much as a car—$30,000.

How do rare animals get to pet shops? First they are stolen from the wild. Poor villagers know just where to look for a baby monkey or a wild bird. Smugglers pay only a few dollars for the animals. Then they are taken out of the country. They go to places where they are sold for a high price. Thieves hide animals in clever ways. Some hide live birds in tennis ball cans! Others tape lizards under their shirts.

The U.S. is working with other countries to stop this. In 1998, a big reptile trader was arrested. But the best way to stop smuggling is simple. Don't buy an endangered animal!

Jorge Picon works for the U.S. Fish and Wildlife Service in Miami, Florida. He tries to keep rare animals out of pet stores. "Every shipment I see breaks my heart," he says. "These animals belong in the wild."

For Sale: Stolen Rare Pets *(cont.)*

Directions: Answer these questions. You may look at the story.

1. What is being stolen?

2. Where do the animals come from?

3. How do smugglers hide them?

4. How could pet stores be discouraged from selling rare animals?

5. Explain why having rare pets is so bad.

6. Why do you think a person would want a rare pet rather than a typical pet?

7. What do you think will happen to rare animals if people continue to smuggle them?

8. Why does Picon's heart break about this?

For Sale: Stolen Rare Pets *(cont.)*

Directions: Using information from the article, add two subtopics to each topic on the web below.

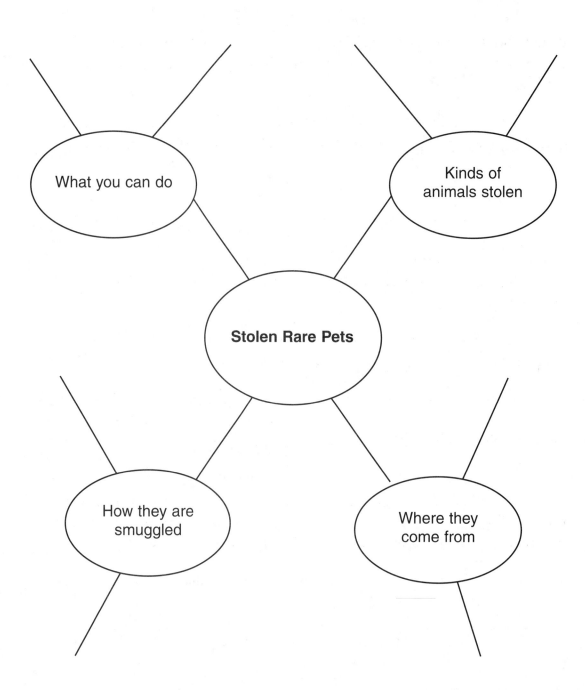

Directions: Read the story.

Great Ball of Fire!

The sun seems to be a quiet ball of light and heat. It warms our skin. It helps plants grow. But this star is hard to understand. It is a loudly exploding ball of fiery gas. Sometimes it whips up big storms on its surface.

This weather can cause problems on Earth. Solar storms can make compass needles point the wrong way. They can even knock out electric and phone service.

Tools are now used to "look inside" the sun. A weatherman can predict rain and snow on the earth. Someday they may be able to forecast storms on the sun.

SOHO is a spacecraft packed with telescopes. It circles the sun taking pictures.

Scientists were surprised by what they found. SOHO found things under the surface of the sun. They found rivers and winds of super hot gas.

Scientists will learn even more of the sun's secrets. In 1997, NASA launched another craft. It tracks the solar wind. These are fiery particles of the sun. They fly through the solar system. They affect weather on the planets.

Scientists hope to predict solar weather. They will learn its effects on Earth. "We used to think the inside of the sun was fairly simple," says Arizona astronomer John Harvey. "But that was before we had the capability to see into it."

Great Ball of Fire! (cont.)

Directions: Answer these questions. You may look at the story.

1. What has been learned about weather on the sun?

2. What problems can solar storms cause?

3. What do astronomers want to predict?

4. What are different uses of a telescope?

5. Compare the job of an astronomer to the job of a weatherman.

6. What does SOHO do?

7. How is solar wind different from wind on Earth?

8. Why would it be helpful to predict weather on the sun?

Great Ball of Fire! *(cont.)*

Directions: Read the information. Answer the questions.

Did You Know?

- More than 1.3 million Earths could fit inside the sun.

- The surface temperature of the sun is 11,000 degrees Fahrenheit.

- The temperature at its center is 57 million degrees Fahrenheit.

- The sun's size and temperature are average compared to those of some of the other 100 billion stars in our galaxy.

- The sun releases bursts of gas called solar flares. Some are larger than 10 Earths.

---

1. Would you say that this display is a diagram, a fact sheet, or a map?

2. Why would an author use this format to provide information? Why weren't the facts just included in the article?

3. How does this information add to the article?

4. Read the first fact. How could this fact be displayed using another kind of visual aid (a map, a graph, etc.)?

Hot on Lewis and Clark's Trail

Nobody likes a litterbug. But historians wish that Lewis and Clark had left more behind. They traveled across the country 200 years ago. It was a trip from Missouri to the Pacific. But it's hard to tell where they stopped on their trip.

Many people are hot on the trail of the explorers. They hope to answer questions about them.

In 1803, the president asked Lewis to go exploring. He was to inspect the Louisiana Purchase. This was a huge area of land. America was about to buy it from France. He hoped to find a water way between the Mississippi River and the Pacific. This would help trade.

Lewis made the trip with his best friend. He and Clark left in May, 1804. They never found the water way. But they were able to see many of America's wonders. They saw the Great Plains. They saw the Rocky Mountains and the Pacific. They faced many perils. There were bear attacks. The weather was bitter cold. In Montana, they carried heavy canoes for weeks around waterfalls. They had to walk through the hot sun. At times, they were very hungry. Some days, they had to eat their pack horses.

Finally, they reached the Pacific. It took 500 days and 4,000 miles. "Ocian in view! O! the joy!" Clark wrote in his journal. (He was a terrible speller.)

The men kept maps and diaries. They wrote about the animals and plants they found. They also wrote about many native tribes. But, they left barely a trace at their campsites. That makes it hard for people to say, "Lewis and Clark were right here!"

Many people hope to pin down such facts. They are digging in the soil at Great Falls and Fort Clatsop. This is where they rested before going their separate ways home. Beads and gun ammunition were recently found at Fort Clatsop. More tests are needed to prove they belonged to Lewis and Clark.

The 200th anniversary of the trip is coming soon. People will be able to learn about the pioneers. PBS will show a film about two men who retraced the trip. A Lewis and Clark museum will open in Great Falls. Celebrations along the trail are in the works.

Hot on Lewis and Clark's Trail *(cont.)*

Directions: Answer these questions. You may look at the story.

1. Who asked Lewis to go exploring?

2. Who did Lewis invite to go with him?

3. What do historians wish they could find?

4. How do you think a water way between the Mississippi and the Pacific would have helped trade?

5. Why do you think it was so important that the explorers described the plants and animals they saw?

6. In what way do you think the maps and diaries were helpful to others?

7. If you were to go on an exploration, what kinds of supplies would you bring?

8. Why do you think this exploration is still celebrated today?

Hot on Lewis and Clark's Trail *(cont.)*

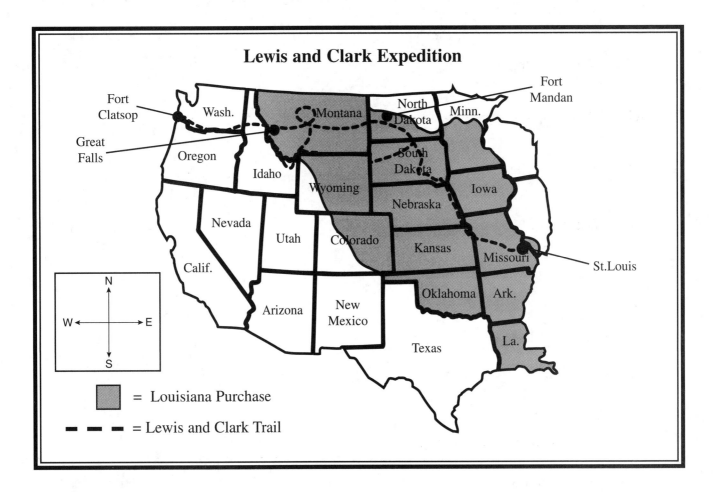

Lewis and Clark Expedition

(Map labels: Fort Clatsop, Great Falls, Wash., Oregon, Idaho, Montana, Wyoming, Nevada, Calif., Utah, Colorado, Arizona, New Mexico, Texas, North Dakota, South Dakota, Nebraska, Kansas, Oklahoma, Minn., Fort Mandan, Iowa, Missouri, St. Louis, Ark., La.)

N / W / E / S

⬛ = Louisiana Purchase

▬ ▬ ▬ = Lewis and Clark Trail

1. What does the shaded portion of the map represent?

2. How much of the Lewis and Clark expedition was spent exploring the area of the Louisiana Purchase?

3. What can you learn from looking at this map of the expedition?

4. How does this map add to your understanding of the article?

5. Look at the trail Lewis and Clark followed. Why do you think this is considered such an important expedition?

What a Winter!

The Ewen family awoke to a scary sight. A nearby creek was spilling over its banks. Soon the waters circled their home. They had to wade through deep water to get out.

"I didn't expect it to come up that fast," says Melissa Ewen. The last time she saw their home, it was nearly covered with water. "Everything we own was in there—photos that can't be replaced."

During the winter of 1997–1998, strong winter storms slammed much of the U.S. Bad weather often hits at this time of year. This time there was a change in climate patterns. It was called El Niño and it made the storms even more dangerous than usual.

El Niño caused strange weather all over the world. "This is the weather event of the century," said James Baker.

Heavy rain began to hit California on February 1. The rain caused flash floods. There were even mudslides. Huge waves crashed over beaches. Winds knocked out power to thousands of homes.

At the same time, thunderstorms and tornadoes roared across Florida. They tossed around trees, roofs, and even small planes. Winds gusted to 100 miles an hour.

Then the storms moved north. Snow, rain, and wind battered much of the East Coast.

Scientists had been studying El Niño. They knew the wild weather would come. El Niño happens every few years. It is caused by winds and ocean currents traveling across the Pacific Ocean.

El Niño causes strange weather all over. Places that usually have a lot of rain may have droughts. Places that have little rain end up with flooding. This El Niño was the strongest one of the century.

El Niño affects more than weather. It warms up large bands of water in the Pacific. This confuses many living things. Fish and birds travel too far north. Sea lions in California starved. The fish they eat swam south.

El Niño was at its strongest in December. Much of the world felt its effects for months.

What a Winter! *(cont.)*

Directions: Answer these questions. You may look at the story.

1. What scary sight did the family wake up to?

2. How did they escape?

3. What causes El Niño?

4. What can scientists learn by studying El Niño?

5. Compare the different kinds of strange weather caused by El Niño.

6. What problems did El Niño cause for animals?

7. What do you think are the good things about the weather El Niño brings?

8. How do you think the author feels about the effects of El Niño?

 ©Teacher Created Materials, Inc.

What a Winter! *(cont.)*

Directions: Look at the map. Answer the questions.

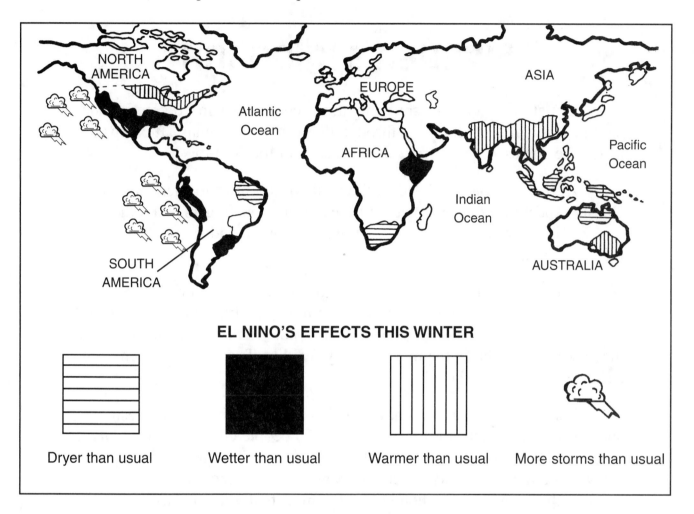

1. What is the purpose of this map?

2. What two things does this map show about the weather patterns from El Niño in the U.S.?

3. How do you think South Africa was affected by El Niño?

4. What does this map show you about the way El Niño affected the world?

Directions: Read the story.

Sweden's Igloo Inn

Sometimes on a very chilly night, the cold creeps in. It creeps under the thickest blankets. It creeps through the warmest pajamas. It creeps inside the coziest socks. Brrrr! It finds a set of toes to nip.

At the Ice Hotel in Sweden, the cold doesn't have to sneak in. Guests expect the cold to nip at their toes. And their fingers. And their noses. That's because the entire hotel is made of ice and snow. Even the furniture is made of ice.

Why would anyone spend money to stay in a snow fort? Its beauty attracts many guests. Guests who stay the night receive a printed Ice Hotel Certificate. It proves they have beaten the cold. The manager says, "After they spend the night, in the morning they feel like Tarzan or He-Man because they slept in there."

For eight years, a shiny new Ice Hotel has been built from fresh ice and snow each winter. Last year about 4,000 people checked in for a night at the Ice Hotel. Guests pay an $80 room charge. They get extra warm snowsuits and mummy-style sleeping bags. Guests need all the extra padding they can get. The hotel's "beds" are actually ice blocks covered with reindeer skins! One hotel visitor said she started to have second thoughts about spending the night there. "It's freezing!" she said. "Apparently everybody makes out O.K. But after I saw the beds, I got a little worried."

By May, warmer temperatures will melt the hotel. But it's not gone for good. Builders start chipping away at another Ice Hotel in October.

     ©*Teacher Created Materials, Inc.*

Sweden's Igloo Inn (cont.)

Directions: Answer these questions. You may look at the story.

1. What is different about the hotel?

2. Where is the hotel?

3. What things at the hotel are made of ice and snow?

4. If you were going to stay at the Ice Hotel, what would you bring to keep warm?

5. How many months during the year do you think the hotel is open? Why?

6. What do people receive after staying at the hotel?

7. Why did seeing the beds make the woman worried?

8. Why do you think people want to stay at the hotel?

Sweden's Igloo Inn (cont.)

Directions: Look at the map. Answer the questions.

1. The Ice Hotel is located inside the Arctic Circle. Write an X in the area where the Ice Hotel is probably located.

2. Canada also has an ice hotel. Why do you think there is not an ice hotel in the United States?

3. What is one other country that could probably build an ice hotel that would stay frozen for several months.

See Africa by Bike

You are invited to set out on a journey. It is across East Africa. You will trek through thick jungles. You will ride through hot deserts. You will cross the Serengeti Plain. Lions, elephants, and zebras roam there. You will climb snowy Mount Kilimanjaro. That is the highest peak in Africa. Along the way you will meet scientists and animal experts. You may even have the chance to solve problems hurting Africa's land and wildlife.

Dan Buettner will join you. He is the leader of the trip. His team will make the trip on mountain bikes. It will last six weeks and cover 1,500 miles. Their packs will weigh 100 pounds. They will be loaded with laptop computers and supplies. They will ride 60 miles a day and camp out at night. Your trail plans are very easy. You will tag along on the Internet.

Buettner has set three world records for bicycling. Six years ago, he began to work with scientists. His travels can be found by kids on the Internet. Each trip can be followed at his Web site. For a fee, a class can take a more active role. They can e-mail the group and ask questions. They can even vote for what route the team should take.

Buettner led an exploration in Central America. They went to a Mayan civilization. Kids helped scientists figure out the population of an ancient city. Buettner tells young explorers, "Your ideas count and may lead to some great discoveries!"

See Africa by Bike *(cont.)*

Directions: Answer these questions. You may look at the story.

1. To what continent are you invited?

2. How can you go on this trip?

3. Who is Dan Buettner?

4. The trip will last six weeks and cover 1,500 miles. How many miles a week would they travel?

5. Why would a class want to pay a fee on the Web site?

6. If you could really go on a bike trip, where would you go? Why?

7. What problems do you think are hurting Africa's land and wildlife?

8. Why do you think Buettner wants kids to know that their ideas count?

See Africa by Bike (cont.)

Directions: Look at the map. Answer the questions.

1. What is the purpose of this map?

2. Why do you think that two countries on the map are shaded?

3. Where is the Serengeti Plain located? (Be specific.)

4. How does this map help you to better understand the article?

Directions: Read the story.

Elephants Talk to Her

In 1984, Katy Payne went to a zoo in Portland, Oregon. Payne is a biologist. She wanted to listen to elephants. All she heard was the boom of giant feet hitting the ground. She also heard a few deep grunts. Payne had a feeling that the elephants were talking to each other. Then she had a memory of being a kid. She was standing near the organ during choir practice. "When the organ played low notes, you could feel it much better than you could hear it." She felt a similar vibration when she stood near the elephants. "It occurred to me that they might be making very powerful, very low-pitched sounds."

She taped the elephants' sounds. Then she played the tapes at fast speeds so that the sounds would be higher. This makes it possible for humans to hear. There they were! She could here the elephants' voices! She spent the next seven years in Africa. She was listening to elephants in the wild.

Payne is an acoustic biologist. This is a scientist who studies the sounds of animals.

She began studying whale communication when she graduated from college. Whales also use sounds with different meanings to talk to each other. But whales string sounds together. They make a pattern with the sounds. Elephants use each sound by itself.

What are the elephants saying? "Most of the calls are group calls," she says. "I think they mean, 'We're here.'"

But elephants can no longer say, "We're here," in many parts of Africa. They've been hunted. People want their ivory tusks. They have been crowded out of their homes, too. Payne thinks that we should open their ears to the language of elephants. Then more people would want to protect them. "Elephants will speak for themselves, if you give them a chance," she says.

 ©Teacher Created Materials, Inc.

Elephants Talk to Her *(cont.)*

Directions: Answer these questions. You may look at the story.

1. What animal does Payne study?

2. Why couldn't the elephant sounds be heard?

3. How did the organ teach Payne about the sounds of elephants?

4. How does a biologist's work help animals?

5. Compare the languages of elephants and whales.

6. What does Payne think the elephants are saying?

7. How can people help the elephants?

8. What is the purpose of this story?

Elephants Talk to Her *(cont.)*

Directions: Look at the chart. Answer the questions.

Sound pitches can be high or low. The human ear has a range of pitches that it can hear. Some animals can hear higher sounds. Some can hear lower sounds.

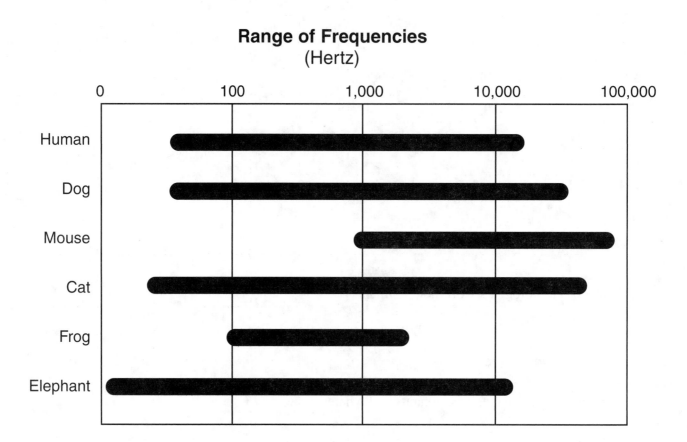

Range of Frequencies
(Hertz)

1. Which animals can hear higher sounds than humans?

2. Which animal can hear the lowest sounds?

3. How does this chart help you to better understand the article?

Student Achievement Graph

Passage Title	Number of Questions Correctly Answered							
	1	2	3	4	5	6	7	8

Answer Key

Page 17
1. South America
2. There was a flood.
3. They were fossilized and found later.
4. Responses will vary.
5. They were able to see parts of the dinosaurs and learn about them.
6. They would have rotted or deteriorated.
7. They were the same size and shape.
8. Responses will vary.
9. Responses will vary.

Page 18
1. Responses will vary. They could probably tell it was a plant eater by its teeth.
2. It was small compared to other dinosaurs that were much larger.

Page 20
1. a tornado
2. They were out in the open and there was no shelter.
3. wind, dark clouds, temperature dropped, no animals in sight
4. Responses will vary.
5. Responses will vary.
6. Responses will vary.
7. Responses will vary.
8. Responses will vary.

Page 21
1. Responses will vary.
2. It would depend on which part of the state you live. In eastern Colorado you would be more likely to experience a tornado than in western Colorado, where it is likely.
3. No. If tornadoes developed over the ocean, then states on the coast would be among the hardest hit.
4. It is a long stretch of land that is shaped like an alley.

Page 23
1. insects
2. 250 tons
3. They eat insects that destroy crops.
4. They eat bugs. They spread pollen. This helps create food for other animals.
5. 750 tons
6. They don't usually hurt people. Usually people hurt them.
7. Responses will vary.
8. Responses will vary.

Page 24
1. Responses will vary.
2. Responses will vary. Answers might include that the diagram shows the bat's anatomy; that the bat hangs upside down; that the bat has four fingers and a thumb like a person, etc.
3. Responses will vary.
4. Responses will vary. The student should list at least three questions.

Page 26
1. helmets
2. He or she is fined $17.
3. The person must show proof that a helmet was purchased.
4. Responses will vary.
5. Responses will vary.

6. Responses will vary.
7. Responses will vary.
8. Responses will vary.

Page 27
1. The map shows which states have passed helmet laws, which have not passed helmet laws, and which states are working on helmet laws.
2. Responses will vary. Answers might include that there are more states that have not passed helmet laws than those that have.
3. Responses will vary.
4. Responses will vary. Answers might suggest that states with higher populations have had more bicycle-related injuries.

Page 29
1. the Great Red Spot
2. a force that pulls toward a planet
3. dust
4. It is the biggest planet.
5. Its gravity isn't strong enough to pull in comets and space rocks.
6. Jupiter is larger and has stronger gravity. Jupiter has rings. Jupiter has several moons. They are both planets. They both have a moon. They both revolve around the sun.
7. Responses will vary.
8. Earth's moon is very large compared to the size of the Earth.

Page 30
1. They are moons.
2. He couldn't see the other moons because his telescope was not powerful enough.

Page 32
1. stop-smoking ads
2. kids
3. Their lungs are damaged.
4. Responses will vary.
5. Responses will vary.
6. Responses will vary.
7. Responses will vary.
8. Responses will vary.

Page 33
1. The graph shows the rate of teen smoking in the United States.
2. The rate of teen smoking increased from '91 to '97.
3. Responses will vary.
4. Responses will vary.
5. The line would go down.

Page 35
1. 27 men
2. They wanted to be the first to travel across Antarctica.
3. They played cards.
4. Responses will vary.
5. Responses will vary.
6. They are small ice houses (igloos for dogs).
7. Responses will vary.
8. Responses will vary.

Page 36
1. It isn't possible to tell. More information is needed.
2. It would be necessary to know from

which continent they started.
3. The shortest route would be from South America.

Page 38
1. high cereal prices
2. about 50 cents
3. make fancy boxes, run ads, include prizes
4. Customers are angry. They want more people to buy their cereal, and angry customers don't.
5. about $3.50
6. They make more money and there are no lower priced choices.
7. Responses will vary.
8. Responses will vary.

Page 39
1. The graph shows the costs involved in making and selling a box of cereal.
2. 41 cents
3. There is a lot of money spent on advertising, paying workers, and paying grocery stores.
4. Responses will vary.

Page 41
1. in Africa
2. twice a month
3. It is too far away.
4. They don't have to drink often. They have wide, flat hooves. They can carry heavy loads.
5. 24 trips
6. Responses will vary.
7. Responses will vary.
8. Responses will vary.

Page 42
1. Responses will vary. Answers might include that the illustration is attempting to show where Kenya is in relation to the continent of Africa and the world.
2. Africa
3. Responses will vary. It represents the capitol city of Kenya.
4. Responses will vary. They are probably not on the map because the towns are so small.

Page 44
1. They train puppies.
2. They will be sled dogs and race in the Iditarod.
3. love and human touch
4. Answers will include some of the following: cuddle, run around, rub their feet, have them pull small sleds, love them.
5. 100
6. They get their feet checked for injuries during races.
7. Responses will vary.
8. Responses will vary.

Page 45
1. It shows the trail of the Iditarod.
2. Responses will vary.
3. Responses will vary. The path probably has to go around mountains and other obstacles.
4. Responses will vary. The trail is probably not an easy one to travel.
5. Responses will vary.

     ©*Teacher Created Materials, Inc.*

Answer Key (cont.)

Page 47
1. a hurricane
2. heavy rains and mud slides
3. He was buried in mud. His parents died.
4. Their homes were destroyed.
5. 1,800
6. Responses will vary.
7. Responses will vary.
8. Responses will vary.

Page 48
1. It is located between North and South America.
2. Responses will vary. They are shaded to show what areas were hit the hardest by the hurricane.
3. Responses will vary. It shows how exposed these countries are and how easy it would be for a hurricane to hit them.
4. Responses will vary.

Page 50
1. being embarrassed in public
2. a chapter of advice in a book called *Girls Know Best*
3. through a writing contest
4. 38 authors
5. Responses will vary.
6. Responses will vary.
7. Responses will vary.
8. Responses will vary.

Page 51
1. page 13
2. Outdoor Adventures
3. Outdoor Adventures

Page 53
1. 15,000
2. It was a bet.
3. It is a long running race.
4. Responses may vary.
5. There were so many people that some had to wait until those in front of them moved.
6. Responses may vary. They were cold and stiff.
7. Responses may vary. The author describes it as legs turning to rubber and arms turning to wood.
8. Responses may vary.

Page 54
1. It shows the route of the Boston Marathon.
2. The route is in a city because it passes colleges, a train depot, etc.
3. The marathon is 26 miles long.

Page 56
1. a baseball player
2. They wanted to break the home run record.
3. Roger Maris
4. No, that's why this was so exciting.
5. They probably practice a lot.
6. They wanted him to break the record. Responses may vary.
7. Responses may vary.
8. Responses may vary.

Page 57
1. It shows the number of home runs hit during the season through August (but not the final number hit that year).
2. Maris was the record holder and the three other players were closest to breaking the record.
3. Each pattern represents a different player.
4. They are tied.

Page 59
1. islands of the Caribbean, Florida, Puerto Rico
2. billions of dollars (as well as 300 lives)
3. a big storm with heavy rains and strong winds
4. Answers may include bend trees, cause floods, crash boats, break power lines, destroy homes, and kill people.
5. Responses may vary.
6. They were told to leave. They needed to find safety.
7. His house was damaged, not destroyed.
8. Responses may vary.

Page 60
1. It spins in the opposite direction of the hands on a clock.
2. The eye is the spot in the center of the hurricane.
3. It will probably stop when it hits the main land of the United States.

Page 62
1. in the ocean
2. home
3. They swim peacefully and playfully with other fish.
4. Some have a long way to get back to where they were born.
5. fishing, pollution, habitat destruction
6. Responses may vary.
7. They need clean water, shade, and a safe home.
8. Responses may vary.

Page 63
1. It shows the life cycle of a salmon.
2. It shows the different stages that the fish goes through in its life.
3. The cycle continues and continues. There is no stopping point.
4. Responses will vary. Answers may suggest that there isn't always one stage at which life begins. Does a fish's life begin when it is born or when the egg is laid or when the adult lays the egg? The diagram shows that all stages are equally important in the life of a salmon.

Page 65
1. food choices between fast food and regular food
2. fast food
3. fries and shakes
4. It is high in fat. Responses may vary.
5. Responses may vary.
6. Responses may vary.
7. Responses may vary.
8. Responses may vary.

Page 66
1. bread, meat, fat, dairy
2. Fruits and vegetables are missing.
3. Responses will vary. Answers should include a combination of the food categories.

Page 68
1. It froze.
2. 62 degrees below zero
3. They have to deal with it a lot.
4. It gets thick and gunky.
5. To keep them warm so their cars will run in the morning.
6. Responses may vary.
7. Responses may vary.
8. Responses may vary.

Page 69
1. Responses may vary.
2. Barrow and Fairbanks
3. Ben probably lives in the central to northern part of the state.

Page 71
1. It floods.
2. a dam
3. to make electricity
4. They will lose their homes. Animals and their habitats will be lost.
5. the people
6. Responses may vary.
7. Responses may vary.
8. Responses may vary.

Page 72
1. It shows where the dam will be built.
2. Responses may vary although Chongqing, Wuhan, Nanjing, and Shanghai are all along the river.

Page 74
1. cattle and sheep
2. the government
3. They starved because there were too many elk for the available food.
4. angry, afraid
5. Responses may vary.
6. Responses may vary.
7. He wants to keep wolves in Yellowstone.
8. Responses may vary.

Page 75
1. It shows a close-up of Wyoming and then it shows where Wyoming is in relation to the whole United States.
2. Responses may vary. Wolves are probably also in Idaho and Montana.
3. Responses may vary.

Page 77
1. a fisherman
2. The fisherman froze it.
3. It was dead.
4. Responses may vary.
5. It is nearly complete.
6. It has short arms.
7. They live deep in the ocean.
8. Responses may vary.

Answer Key (cont.)

Page 78
1. Responses will vary. A squid has one fin and fish have more. Fish do not have tentacles. A fish does not squirt ink.
2. Responses will vary.
3. Responses will vary.
4. Responses will vary.
5. It shows the parts of a squid, that it has suckers, feeds with its tentacles, can have large eyes, etc.

Page 80
1. gas, coal, oil
2. They are fuels that come from plants and animals that died millions of years ago.
3. wind and sun
4. Responses may vary.
5. Responses may vary.
6. They are not limited sources.
7. Responses may vary.
8. Responses may vary.

Page 81
1. Water power is not discussed.
2. Responses may vary.

Page 83
1. A local river is polluted.
2. He wants the president to get the rivers cleaned up.
3. refrigerator, dead cow, pop cans
4. nearby
5. Responses may vary.
6. Responses may vary.
7. Responses may vary.
8. to convince people that we should take care of rivers

Page 84
1. An outline assists in planning and organizing writing.
2. Responses may vary.

Page 86
1. in the Atlantic Ocean
2. He was captured.
3. bad living conditions, pool too small and warm
4. Healthy whales have glossy skin and straight fins. Keiko's skin had sores and his dorsal fin flopped over.
5. He went to a better aquarium and was given the care he needed.
6. Responses may vary.
7. He gained 2,000 pounds and his sores went away.
8. Responses may vary.

Page 87
1. Responses will vary.
2. Responses will vary.
3. It has a whale in the center of it.
4. about 4,575 miles

Page 89
1. rare animals
2. jungles
3. They put them in tennis ball cans or tape them under clothes.
4. Responses may vary.
5. Responses may vary.
6. Responses may vary.
7. They could become extinct. Responses may vary.
8. Responses may vary.

Page 90
Web subtopics will vary.

Page 92
1. It is stormy.
2. They can cause problems with compasses, electricity, and phone service.
3. weather on the sun
4. Responses may vary.
5. Responses may vary.
6. SOHO takes pictures of the sun.
7. Wind on Earth is blowing air. Solar wind is made of fiery particles of the sun.
8. Responses may vary.

Page 93
1. It is a fact sheet.
2. Responses will vary.
3. Responses will vary.
4. Responses will vary. The fact could be displayed in the form of a diagram, showing Earth's size compared to the sun.

Page 95
1. the president
2. his friend, Clark
3. more information about the explorer's trip
4. Responses may vary.
5. Responses may vary.
6. Responses may vary.
7. Responses may vary.
8. Responses may vary.

Page 96
1. It represents the Louisiana Purchase.
2. Most of it was spent exploring the area of the Lousiana Purchase. Only the travels through Idaho, Washington, and Oregon were not a part of the Louisiana Purchase.
3. Responses will vary.
4. Responses will vary.
5. Responses will vary. It covered such a large area that had not been explored by Americans or Europeans before that time.

Page 98
1. They awoke to flooding around their house.
2. They waded through deep water.
3. winds and ocean currents in the Pacific
4. They can tell when the weather is coming.
5. There are heavy rains vs. droughts.
6. They got confused. Fish and birds went too far north or south. Sea lions starved because their food (the fish) wasn't available.
7. Responses may vary.
8. Responses may vary.

Page 99
1. It shows the parts of the world that were affected by El Niño.
2. The southwest was wetter than usual. The northeast was warmer than usual.
3. Responses will vary. There was less rain, so crops might have been affected.
4. Responses will vary.

Page 101
1. It is made of ice and snow.
2. in Sweden
3. everything
4. Responses may vary.
5. Probably only six or seven months. The sun melts it when the weather gets warm.
6. a certificate
7. Responses may vary.
8. Responses may vary.

Page 102
1. The X should be drawn on Sweden inside the Arctic Circle.
2. Responses may vary.
3. Russia could probably have an ice hotel. The U.S. could probably build one in Alaska.

Page 104
1. Africa
2. on the Internet
3. He is a bicyclist and trip leader.
4. 250 miles a week
5. They can participate more and interact with the team.
6. Responses may vary.
7. Responses may vary.
8. Responses may vary.

Page 105
1. It shows the area where the bike team will be.
2. Responses will vary. These are the countries where the team will be.
3. It is located in both Kenya and Tanzania.
4. Responses will vary.

Page 107
1. the elephant
2. They were too low for the human ear.
3. She remembered that the low notes on the organ could be felt better than heard.
4. Responses may vary.
5. Whales string sounds together. Elephants' sounds are separate.
6. "We're here!"
7. Responses may vary.
8. To teach people and to persuade them to help elephants.

Page 108
1. dogs, mice, cats
2. the elephant
3. Responses may vary.